PATTERNS FOR WORSHIP

A Report by the Liturgical Commission
of the General Synod of the Church of England

GS 898

This Report has only the authority of the Commission by which it was prepared.

CHURCH HOUSE PUBLISHING
Church House, Great Smith Street, London SW1P 3NZ

ISBN 0 7151 3727 1

Published 1989 for the General Synod of the Church of England by Church House Publishing.

GS 898

See also under Acknowledgements, px.

Printed by Tasprint Limited, South Woodford, London E18 1HB.

CONTENTS

APPENDICES

PREFATORY NOTE

by the House of Bishops

Particular attention is drawn to Paragraph 8 of this Note.

1 The Report *Patterns for Worship* has been produced by the Liturgical Commission in response to the House of Bishops' agreement (June 1986) that the Commission

> should proceed to prepare a handbook(s) which aimed:
>
> (a) to provide some indication of different ways of doing liturgy, taking into account sociological, architectural and churchmanship differences.
>
> (b) to indicate where advantage might be taken of notes and rubrics in the ASB to develop and enrich the liturgy.
>
> (c) to provide outline structures and mandatory sections for some main services, which, if authorised alongside ASB, would provide greater freedom for those who wish either to enrich or shorten the services (including 'family' services and worship in UPAs).

2 That agreement by the House of Bishops was made in consequence of two debates in the General Synod. In November 1985 Synod took note of the report *The Worship of the Church* (GS 698), and in February 1986 it welcomed the report *Faith in the City,* commending it to the Church for 'study, discussion and action'. In *The Worship of the Church,* para. 40, the Standing Committee had suggested

> a programme of study and discussion . . . and a 'directory' with a wealth of resource materal including supplementary material for each of the many points in the service where there is room for the individual's own words. The directory would need to set boundaries to the proposed freedom and points which might be theologically divisive would have to be watched. Yet it could give encouragement to the 'loosening up' which the ASB 1980 clearly had in mind but of which real advantage is yet to be taken.

Faith in the City reported (para. 6.110):

> Many submissions included suggestions about books, services and groups. As we noted in Chapter 3 to give people a 1300 page Alternative Service Book is a symptom of the gulf between the Church and ordinary people in the UPAs.

We have heard calls for short, functional service booklets or cards, prepared by people who will always ask 'if all the words are really necessary'. The work of re-forming the Liturgy has really only just begun for the UPA Church, and we recommend that the Liturgical Commission pay close attention to the needs of Churches in the UPAs.

3 Since June 1986 there have been other requests relating to Liturgy to which the Liturgical Commission offers the attached Report as its response.

(i) The Report *Children in the Way* (received February 1988) called upon the Liturgical Commission to

examine the need for new liturgies to serve all-age worship and in particular for a form of Eucharist suitable for when children are present.

(ii) The Report *Called to be Adult Disciples* (GS 794) (received November 1987)

welcomed the flexibility provided in the Alternative Services book and recommended that each parish find ways of affirming lay vocations within its liturgy . . . [and that] the Liturgical Commission produces material which values and celebrates the daily lives and experiences of lay people.

(iii) A motion passed at a separate session of the House of Laity of the General Synod in February 1988 asked that steps be taken towards

ensuring in our parishes an adequate provision of non-eucharistic as well as eucharistic services.

4 In preparing *Patterns for Worship* the Commission has endeavoured to consult widely. And in particular it has, with the required archiepiscopal sanction, made use of the power conferred by Canon B 5A for a minister to conduct a draft service in the presence of a designated congregation, in order to test out some of its material in urban parishes of varying traditions and regional locations.

5 The House of Bishops has recognised these various and urgently expressed calls for liturgical proposals – and the widely based consultations which the Commission has undertaken. However, the House is mindful of those who want a period of stability in the liturgical life of the Church, and who might beanxious lest

the Commission's proposals extend the bounds of choice and variety of liturgical provision more widely than has been customary in the Church of England. Much of the material in *Patterns for Worship* is designed for use in situations where freedom to use 'other alternative words' already exists and is freely taken. Yet, as the Report indicates, there are some proposals, particularly for new alternative Eucharistic Prayers, which could only be authorised for use after due process of liturgical business and approval in the General Synod.

The House has particularly noted those aspects of the Commission's proposals which could, by widening the scope of that which is allowed within statutory services, be a reining-in of the unco-ordinated, unauthorised and unstructured provisions which are now widespread in the context of non-statutory services.

It will be noted that the Commission's proposals for authorisation envisage the variation of the rubrics in the ASB Eucharist and Morning and Evening Prayer to permit the use of approved material within the existing ASB structures. One important consequence of this would be to bring new material within the ambit of the 1974 Worship and Doctrine Measure, thereby engaging PCCs in discussion and decision on the appropriate style and content of worship in their situation, and the frequency and blend in which new and existing texts might be used.

6 The Constitution of the Liturgical Commission requires it 'to prepare forms of service at the request of the House of Bishops for submission to that House in the first instance', and also 'to advise on the experimental use of forms of service duly authorised by the General Synod'.

7 The House of Bishops, having received the Report, now agrees to its publication as a General Synod paper so that the process of discussion and comment on what is proposed can be widened *before any authorisation or commendation such as to allow the proposals to be used liturgically is given.* In due course the House hopes that there may be a general wide-ranging 'take note' debate in the General Synod. After there has been such a debate and period of discussion the House will reflect upon it, and then determine whether it wishes to bring forward material for Synodical authorisation and whether to commend resource material in the Report for use in contexts where full authorisation is not required.

8 Particular attention is therefore drawn to the customary disclaimer on the title page that 'this report has only the authority of the Commission by which it was prepared', and it is to be emphasised that no part of the material contained in the Report is yet authorised or commended for liturgical use.

On behalf of the House
ROBERT CANTUAR:
July 1989 *Chairman*

MEMBERS OF THE COMMISSION

The Rt Revd Colin James, Bishop of Winchester *(Chairman)*

The Revd Dr Mark Dalby
Mrs Molly Dow (from November 1987)
The Ven. Trevor Lloyd, Archdeacon of Barnstaple
The Revd Michael Perham
The Revd Dr Geoffrey Rowell
The Ven. David Silk, Archdeacon of Leicester
The Revd Jane Sinclair
The Rt Revd William Persson, Bishop of Doncaster
(from November 1987)
The Revd Dr Bryan Spinks
The Very Revd David Stancliffe, Provost of Portsmouth
The Revd Dr Kenneth Stevenson
The Revd Canon John Sweet
The Revd Michael Vasey
Miss Jinny Wade

Consultant
Mr Robin Brookes

Secretary
Mr David Hebblethwaite

The Rt Revd Michael Baughen, Bishop of Chester (resigned September 1987) and Mr Adrian Scott (resigned March 1987) were original members of the Commission appointed in 1986.

ACKNOWLEDGEMENTS

The Liturgical Commission wishes to record its indebtedness to churches, publishers and individuals whose texts have been made available for inclusion in *Patterns for Worship*, either in original or in adapted form.

Among published sources, mention should be made particularly of the following:–

Anglican Church of Canada: *The Book of Alternative Services* (1985)

Church of the Province of New Zealand: *A New Zealand Prayer Book* (1989)

Anglican Church of Australia: *An Australian Prayer Book* (1978)

The Society of St Francis: *The Daily Office SSF* (1981)

Some use has been made of revised service books of the Church of Ireland, the Episcopal Church in the USA, and the Scottish Episcopal Church.

Among those who have made local material available, particular thanks are due to Portsmouth Cathedral; Westcott House, Cambridge; Holy Trinity, Guildford, and Holy Trinity, Wealdstone.

1 INTRODUCTION

WHY A NEW BOOK?

The coming of the Alternative Service Book in 1980 marked a new stage in the development of Anglican worship. In one sense the ASB looked back four hundred years to the principle established by Cranmer of having all the texts for worship available in one book: the ASB gathered and distilled the best of all the little experimental booklets of the years since 1965, summing up and, some hoped, ending that period of experimentation.

But in another sense the Alternative Service Book looked forward to a new era of flexibility in the Church of England worship. At many points the text provided alternative options or open-ended phrases such as 'using these or other appropriate words', 'these or other suitable words', 'or other suitable prayers'. In Rite A such phrases govern the opening welcome, introduction to confession, the form of intercessions, the peace, extra words of distribution, the prayer after communion. This principle, of allowing considerable freedom in some areas of the liturgy where there is no danger of harm or division if people do different things, was extended in the services in the 1985 book *Lent, Holy Week, Easter*. The provision for the *Agape* in that book, for instance, is basically a list of instructions about how to do it and where to go for texts.

Our aim in producing *Patterns for Worship* is to meet some of the current needs of the Church's worship, reflected most acutely in Urban Priority Areas and in services (often called 'Family Services') at which all age groups, including children, are present. We have used the already established principle of flexibility to provide forms of worship which will still be part of the Anglican family, while encompassing the enormous variety that exists within the Church at present.

So we have provided three main items:

First, clear outline structures for main services, indicating what must be used and what is entirely flexible. These can easily be used by parishes wishing to produce their own services. We have added (see pp. 31-105) sample ways of doing this, suitable for setting out as service cards with bold type and pictures which might be produced nationally for parishes which do not have the resources to produce their own.

Second, sections of resource material grouped under various headings, roughly in the order in which they might come in a service. An introductory paragraph to each section gives guidance on how to use it, and on how to take advantage of the notes and rubrics in the Alternative Service Book to enrich the liturgy.

Third, a commentary, to show how the structures and resource section might be used, and how worship relates to differences in architecture, churchmanship and cultural background.

Urban Priority Areas

The flexibility of the *Patterns* approach should help us to do what the *Faith in the City* report suggests, in moving away from a 1300-page book for the congregation, and providing for liturgy to 'emerge out of and reflect local cultures'. That report asked for 'short, functional service booklets or cards', and we have provided for these. The report also asked for liturgy that promoted 'a greater involvement of the congregation' and was 'more concrete and tangible than abstract and theoretical', and the new writing we have done, for instance in the new eucharistic prayers, is designed to meet these needs. But the needs of the UPA parish for worship reflecting local culture, language and concrete expression are not best met by a group of experts at the centre laying down all the words of liturgy, but by creating the framework and the environment which will enable a new generation of worship leaders to create genuinely local liturgy which is still obviously part of the liturgy of the catholic Church.

'Family' Services

Many of the same things could be said about 'Family' Services: clear simple structures, concrete language, and responsiveness to local culture and gifts are all necessary. The 'Family Service' in the Church of England varies enormously from place to place. In some places it is but a pale and timid reflection of the standard fare: the Chelmsford report on non-statutory worship, *For the Family*, uses words like 'inhibited and awkward', 'stilted, uncreative and frankly boring' about some services, 'led in a very conservative and staid fashion.' Some of the criticisms of the 'Family Service' voiced in the Church today are:

- Worship is 'childish' and the focus is on children to such an extent that adults are forced to deny their adulthood by joining in.

- It focuses so strongly on the nuclear family that it makes those in other styles of household, the single, bereaved, divorced and elderly, feel less part of the church family.
- Both structure and contents are so free and variable that people see no links with traditional Anglican worship.
- It fails to act as a 'bridge' to more main line eucharistic or Morning Prayer worship: some worshippers never move on from a monthly 'Family Service'.
- Its worship is banal, superficial, dominated by a 'compere' or a strong teaching aim, providing little God-centred worship.
- Worship depends on the whim of the worship leader because so much is new; and because it is not a 'statutory' service, there is sometimes little or no consultation with the PCC.

But in other places the 'Family Service' is the main sign of hope for the Church, reflecting an enormous amount of creative energy and the kind of God-centred worship that is resulting in a considerable growth of new Christians. Many of the points listed above might be countered by a positive list:

- 'Family Service' provides a place where those unfamiliar with formal worship can begin to feel at home.
- One reason for this is that it can be a bridge, in reflecting local culture more easily than the rest of the Church's worship.
- Another reason is that people sometimes welcome the excuse to accompany their children, and then find they understand teaching which is simple and visual, and sometimes at a more 'introductory' level.
- It is a place where genuine intergenerational activity takes place, with adults and children learning from each other in worship.
- It can help regular church attenders to discover new dimensions in worship.
- It provides an opportunity for people to grow and use their gifts by sharing in planning, leading and contributing to worship.
- It provides a way of introducing new elements into worship (in a congregation likely to be less critical of them?) – drama, dance, audiovisuals, new hymns or methods of teaching.

Family

All this begs the question of what we mean by 'family'. Who is the 'Family Service' for? 'Family Service' (or 'Family Communion') is often used as a more folksy title for the Eucharist or Holy Communion, to emphasize that it is for the whole church family every week, or that provision is made for children as well as adults. 'All-age worship' is another title for this, to stress that people of all ages can worship together. But 'Family Service' has also replaced 'Children's Church' as a title, to mean a random collection of adults and children, or a large number of children while Sunday School teachers have a monthly break.

We would want to interpret 'family' in its widest sense. All are daughters or sons; some are sisters, brothers, parents, cousins, grandparents. Some are part of a nuclear family of parents and children, or a single parent family, or a kinship family including grandparents or aunts, or a reconstituted family where parents bring children from previous relationships. Others, with no marriage or blood relationship are part of an intentional family or household, deliberately committed to one another for caring and mutual support, and sometimes for a specific purpose such as being a mission house for the local church. And some families may be mixtures of these different types.

The church family needs to acknowledge and value all of these, and to embrace also those who live alone, or without such immediate family relationships. The church family at worship should acknowledge the presence and gifts of children, and be open to inter-generational learning and experience of worship: it should not be focused exclusively on the needs of the traditional English middle-class nuclear family. And, as the *Children in the Way* report argues, 'family' is not the only model for the church, and can sometimes damage people by appearing to exclude them. For this reason we do not think the title 'Family Service' should be adopted formally by the Church of England, and we look for a more satisfactory alternative to emerge. The 'pilgrim church' model provides some exciting educational (and processional'.) possibilities, but we doubt whether 'Pilgrim Service' would convey the required image'.

Much more could be said about the 'Family Service', such as the need for clear aims for the planning group, and for a regular review of where this Service fits in relation to the rest of the local church's worship. We hope that the *Patterns for Worship* proposals and especially the Service of the Word guidelines will encourage change away from the unhelpful aspects of the 'Family Service', while ensuring that its creative, vibrant life is not locked up in non-statutory, non-eucharistic and mini-family centred worship. It must be part of the living, contemporary tradition of the whole Church's worship.

Common Prayer?

Inevitably, a directory approach such as that in *Patterns for Worship* raises questions about the concept of 'common prayer', and about whether or how doctrinal conformity can be secured. 'Common prayer' does not in fact exist, in the sense of being able to walk into any church in the land and find exactly the same words to follow. Nor should we pretend that it would be either good or right to return to a position - well over a century ago - when that might have been the case. Rather, 'common prayer' exists in the Church of England in the sense of recognizing, as one does when visiting other members of the same family, some common features, some shared experiences, language and patterns or traditions. To accept a variety of forms, dictated by local culture, is part of our Anglican heritage, spelt out by Archbishop Thomas Cranmer in his 1549 Preface: 'it often chanceth diversely in diverse countries'.

What are the marks of Anglican worship that we might expect to find (or have a right to find?) in Family Services or UPA worship. We believe that some of the marks which should be safeguarded for those who wish to stand in any recognizable continuity with historic Anglican tradition are:

– a recognizable structure for worship
– an emphasis on reading the word and on using psalms
– liturgical words repeated by the congregation, some of which, like the creed, would be known by heart
– using a collect, the Lord's Prayer, and some responsive forms in prayer
– a recognition of the centrality of the Eucharist
– a concern for form, dignity, and economy of words: as the four-year old said on TV about Church of England services, 'Now I know churches are true: the people in them enjoy singing and walk about in patterns.'

Another mark of Anglican worship is a willingness to use forms and prayers which can be used across a broad spectrum of Christian belief. This may sometimes mean that, for the sake of the unity of the Church, we refrain from using some words which reflect one of the traditional 'party' positions. Most debates about doctrinal conformity are really about how to stop the other person doing something you don't like because you think it is right on the edge of being heretical. We think the provisions of the Canons sufficiently safeguard this. Canon A 5 states that the doctrine of the Church of England 'is to be found in the Thirty-nine Articles of Religion, the Book of Common Prayer, and the Ordinal.' In other words, these texts represent a doctrinal norm, and nothing in new services, whether approved by the General Synod (Canon B 2), or approved by the Convocations, Archbishops or Ordinary (Canon B 4), or considered suitable, or varied (insubstantially) by the minister (Canon B 5) may be 'contrary to, nor indicative of any departure from the doctrine of the Church of England in any essential matter.' And in the case of the latter two Canons (only'.), the forms of service also have to be reverent and seemly.

But we suggest, both to secure doctrinal orthodoxy and to avoid the divisions caused by 'party' texts, that there should be some parts of the service with a limited number of options. The Service Outlines and notes sometimes indicate that there is a choice only between material in the Book of Common Prayer, the Alternative Service Book, or the Resource Sections. Material covered in this way includes the creed, confession and absolution, specific prayer about the departed, and the eucharistic prayer. There will be some who will think that even this minimum amount of regulation goes counter to what we have said about local creativity, and infringes local control of worship. To them we would point out the traditional function of 'catholic' faith and worship in providing a critique or alternative viewpoint for looking at local (or national) culture.

SERVICE STRUCTURE

A glance at history shows us the pedigree of the different strands of non-eucharistic worship which we find today in the 'Family Service', Morning and Evening Prayer, and the first half of Holy Communion. There are three strands in antiquity: the Word Service (first part of Holy Communion), Daily Prayer (Morning and Evening Prayer), and the Teaching or Instruction. (The evidence here is from the writings of Justin Martyr and the *Apostolic Tradition* of Hippolytus, but it is also to be found in many other places.)

The Word Service in Justin consists of readings from the prophets or memoirs of the Apostles, read for as long as time allowed. This is followed by a discourse, and common prayer. This core of material is still recognizable in all major traditions, even though other elements were added in the intervening centuries. Usually there is an approach, with prayer and praise, and possibly penitence; then the readings, the last of which is a Gospel reading, followed in turn by a sermon, and possibly the creed and intercessions. What sort of 'shape' does this give us? It would be possible to see the climax of such a service either in the reading of the Gospel (even though it is a later addition), or in the intercessions, as the response of faith: the living sacrifice of the Church responding to the Word proclaimed and preached.

The content of daily prayer in Hippolytus' *Apostolic Tradition* is less precise. The emphasis is on the *times* of daily prayer - prayer in the heart, with a few people, or many. The later evidence of East and West suggests that the main times were morning and evening, and the service consisted of praise in fixed psalms, hymns and songs, together with intercession. Later developments saw many introductory prayers, the continuous recitation of the Psalter, and readings from Scripture in ever increasing chunks, with other Christian writings. The earlier heart of daily prayer, praise to God at certain times of the day, came to be lost by the lengthier psalm-singing and readings, and so its structure was distorted.

The 'Teaching' type of service centering on instruction in the Word of God is referred to in the *Apostolic Tradition* and may be a direct offspring of the corresponding synagogue service, a bible study with no particular liturgical shape.

As history proceeds, these three types of service, majoring on reading the word, on prayer and praise, and on teaching, do not remain distinct. By the time Cranmer at the Reformation combines the seven medieval 'hours' into Morning and Evening Prayer, prayer and praise are combined with an emphasis on reading and teaching the Word.

Before we draw some conclusions from this, a further glance at history suggests that Christians in the early Church were not divided up according to *age*, but rather according to *stage*, so that catechumens (those preparing for baptism, however old they were) were excluded from the Eucharist. Their formal departure at the end of the Word Service would have been a dramatic feature of the liturgy in a large building, probably involving some upheaval in the congregation as a whole. Perhaps we might make similar structural provision today. As they did in the early Church, we are again providing (for instance in the Alternative Service Book provision for family baptism) not only for individuals but for whole families to move from a non-Christian to a Christian lifestyle. We should no longer be organizing our church life and worship on the assumption that people grow from being less Christian to more Christian in parallel with their age (and so older people but not children are admitted to communion . . .)

Assumptions about structure

In *Patterns for Worship* we have worked on the basis of some conclusions from this:

First, a clear structure is essential. Its main components should stand out so that worshippers can see the shape, development and climax of the service - so that they 'know where they are going'. It is helpful if this is reflected in the way the service is laid out for printing.

Second, we have regarded 'word-services' of different structures as an interchangeable first part of Holy Communion.

Third, as we see the three different types of service come together in history, and as it is fairly unlikely that a parish would have three different types of the Service of the Word each Sunday, we need a balance in any one service, between prayer and praise, word and teaching. This means we should not have a service which is nothing but teaching, without praise and prayer; nor a service which is nothing but praise, without some word and teaching.

Fourth, in making the distinction between the Service of the Word and the Breaking of Bread, between the first and second parts of the Eucharist, we should allow for a pattern to develop where there is a sufficient break between the two parts (perhaps with an extended Peace, with or without refreshments!), for those enquiring about the Christian faith and baptism to go without embarrassment, at the end of the Service of the Word.

READING THE BIBLE

While the bible-reading part of our worship may sometimes be done well, there is a need for some new approaches. Consider some of the reasons why reading the word of God fails to have the effect it ought to have:

1 The readings are treated as if they were boring. This may sometimes be due to the version used, the length of the reading, or the way in which it is read, as if it were a duty to be done, and not part of the worship.

2 Partial or unhelpful meanings are imposed on the readings, for example by bad introductions. The readings should be intro-

duced in such a way as to help people to listen together, to reflect on their particular situation in the light of the Word. For this reason, we do not think books of 'standard' introductions should be produced.

3 Many churches do not use the lectionary provision, omitting readings and changing them to fit the service theme: sometimes only a few verses are read, to be used as the sermon text. This results in a narrower overall diet of Scripture, sometimes determined by the particular interests of the minister.

4 There is a general devaluing of the practice of listening to Scripture being read, and of reading it well. Readers need training. Even in Family Services it is wrong to have children reading who cannot be heard, or who read without understanding: the same should be true for adults.

5 There is a reluctance to use the Old Testament, even in the Advent to Christmas period when it is the controlling reading.

6 Few people have thought about the reasons for reading the Bible in worship.

7 Congregations suffer from a presentation that is often unimaginative and expects little response.

8 Current lectionary provision is comparatively poor.

We offer three possible solutions:

1 *The Church should rediscover the excitement of reading the Scriptures in worship, as something that makes the people of God what they are.*

This means helping everyone to understand why we read Scripture in worship. We read Scripture not just to teach and instruct, but in order to link us firmly with the tradition, to ensure that we listen to the whole counsel of God, to deliver us from the personal whim or interest of the preacher or worship leader, to allow one part of Scripture to throw kaleidoscopic light on another, to identify ourselves again as the people to whom God is speaking. The Doctrine Commission's *Believing in the Church* report makes the point strongly that by publicly rehearsing its corporate story the community is proclaiming its identity as the people of God. Shared stories bind people together.

If Scripture is there just for teaching purposes, some in the congregation (and ministers as well . . .) easily respond, 'I can think of something better – perhaps not in the Bible – on that theme'. But the readings are not there just to illustrate a theme, or help people think about some piece of teaching. They are there because they are normative to and determinative of Christian faith and experience: they both set the boundaries and have an active, stimulating, energizing effect – releasing energy like a hammer breaking rock in pieces. . . We should encourage congregations to respond to the recitation of the great acts of God (more pauses for meditation, more responses, short prayers or a verse of a psalm after the reading. See the Commentary section on 'The Word'.

2 *Each church should improve its approach to, and presentation of, the readings to encourage the congregation to 'own' them.*

Some churches encourage the congregation to use the Sunday readings for personal meditation during the preceding week, or have them discussed in home groups. Changes in presentation might mean the actual involvement of the congregation, in interjections and responses (or stamping feet as in the synagogue when the story of Haman is read!). The congregation can be involved in both drama and dialogue readings. It might mean changing the visual presentation, removing distractions by putting all lights out apart from a spotlight on the reader, or signalling the fact that a story is being read by using a Jackanory armchair, or that a proclamation (for example Amos?) is being made by using a soapbox. Some of this depends on architecture, space and numbers, and little can be indicated in the lectionary. It is more a matter of using the imagination, though it is possible to give an indication where a long story reading might be broken up, for example by songs, or to show how a dialogue (or other types of Scripture) might be read in parts, as in *The Dramatised Bible*.

3 *The Church of England should make further and more imaginative lectionary provision*

We should note the value of story, and not only in inner urban areas and with children. Narrative is comforting and satisfying, challenging because it involves the hearers, emotionally irreplaceable – a more natural part of our life communication than didactic speech. There would be value in including more story provision in our lectionary:

- it is easy to listen to, identify with, remember and re-tell;
- it links the community clearly with the tradition of God's saving action;

- in worship, it can more easily be used to stimulate praise, as we hear what God has done, rather than receive instruction.
- it is important for children: action stories keep things moving, add a sense of excitement and humanity.

When we examine the Alternative Service Book Sunday lectionary for stories, we find glaring omissions. We have the call of Abraham (twice) but nothing of Lot, Hagar, Ishmael or Isaac. There is nothing from the Joseph saga, Moses in the bullrushes, the plagues, the spies in Canaan, the fall of Jericho, Achan, Deborah, Barak – all excellent story material, easily memorable and good listening even if some are long – are all missing. None of the Samson stories are there. In the New Testament, while we have Peter's declaration, the transfiguration and the raising of Lazarus every year, the only feeding miracle is John 6, and the only part of John 4 is theological dialogue rather than the narrative. Omissions include Mary and Martha, the man born blind, Jesus calming the storm, Legion, the pool of Bethesda, the story of the rich fool.

We should look at ways of changing our current lectionary provision, perhaps by experimenting with a 'closed season' around the main seasons of the Church's year, when a restricted seasonal lectionary would be mandatory, and an 'open season' for the rest of the year with several different options, one of which could clearly be a series of 'storyline' sets of readings. We offer some samples of this approach, in Resource Section 4 on pp. 127-30.

THE EUCHARISTIC PRAYER

Problems

1 The length, sentence structure, and monologue style of the present eucharistic prayers have proved difficult both for UPAs and for situations where large numbers of children are present, such as Family Services. Indeed, anyone who is new to church or inexperienced in liturgy finds both the length and the frequency with which new concepts are introduced difficult.

2 There are requests, for example in the debate on the report *Children in the Way*, for a shorter eucharistic prayer for use with children. We believe it is not right to publish prayers for this specific need until such time as larger numbers of children are actually receiving communion. Our situation is very different from the Roman Catholic Church, where children receive at a younger age and many can do so, for example at school Eucharists. But we

recognize that in many churches children are present without receiving communion, and that what is said needs to be capable of being understood by the whole family at worship. We believe that some of the prayers we have produced may provide what is needed, as they are shorter, use more pictorial and concrete language, and provide responses. In particular, the use of Eucharistic Prayer D with one of the shorter responsive prefaces from the Thanksgiving section may be found suitable.

3 We recognize that there are political, synodical and churchmanship problems which arise as soon as the possibility of change in such a sensitive area is raised. The forces of tradition, inertia, fear of insecurity and upheaval should not be allowed to prevent the continuing growth and development of the liturgy which is necessary to meet the needs of those in our cities, or suburbs, (or countryside . . .)

Some Principles

1 We have recognized and accepted the fact that there is no longer one agreed Eucharistic prayer in the Church of England. Those currently authorized include that in the Book of Common Prayer, two options in Rite B, six options in Rite A (including the order following the Book of Common Prayer and one for use with the sick). There is already authority for omitting part of the thanksgiving in Eucharistic Prayer 2, and for extempore prefaces in the Agape provision in Lent, Holy Week, Easter. We believe there should also be variety in the pattern of the prayer, as well as the contents. There is no one definitive or universally acknowledged historic pattern for the eucharistic prayer. So we have provided three prayers with different patterns, and one (prayer D) which follows the more familiar Rite A pattern but provides for a much wider variety in the content of the thanksgiving. It is impossible to say all there is to say on any one eucharistic occasion, or in any one printed prayer. Variety is essential.

2 We have tried not to produce texts which are divisive, in terms of inclusive language, international unity, or theological or churchmanship divisions. We have used internationally agreed texts for the Sanctus and Benedictus, and kept a standard dialogue. It might help the Church to distinguish between those parts of the eucharistic prayer which are theologically sensitive (finding the right words for the coming of the Spirit, for remembering Christ in such a way as to allow him to be present now, and for re-telling his

words at the Last Supper) and those which are less sensitive. A way might then be found of making the former mandatory (allowing for the use of any authorized text), while encouraging creative variation in other areas, such as the thanksgiving.

3 There should be a trinitarian balance within a eucharistic prayer, but not necessarily a trinitarian pattern. Nor is there any need, especially if the creed has been used earlier, for the thanksgiving to be a credal historical list, the substance of which is repeated in the memorial in our current prayers. The Church should be encouraged to rejoice in the contemporary effects of the historic facts . . .

4 We believe there should be some texts available which are thoroughly responsive, not only to prevent the eucharistic monologue which many find difficult, but to embody our belief that the whole congregation is involved in celebrating the Eucharist.

5 'Consecration' is by the whole prayer and action of the community, and cannot be identified with particular words or a particular stage in the prayer. This means we need not cling to particular forms of words, apart from those which are important for unity. So we would argue that the particular form of the narrative of institution is not so important as some have thought in the past. In the continuing debate on the development of the eucharistic prayer the narrative is regarded as a later insertion (which is not to question its legitimacy) in a sequence of thanksgiving and supplication. We have provided a different shorter form of the narrative for each prayer for two reasons. First, the Scripture records show there are different ways of telling the story of the Last Supper, and we think this should be reflected in the Church's liturgy. Second, each form of the narrative is designed to fit with the style, rhythm, length and sentence structure of one of the prayers.

New Prayers

We have provided four new Eucharistic Prayers, which we believe are capable of being used by the whole Church. All four are trinitarian in balance, but each has a different style and 'feel'.

Eucharistic Prayer A is thoroughly responsive, with a clear presidential role in moving the congregation to make responses which further the action stage by stage. Many of the active words are given to the congregation, as well as worship texts drawn from Revelation which set the action in heaven. The thanksgiving for creation mentions parts of God's creation evident in many cities – hills and river, sun and rain – and the offertory prayers are deliberately included here to link *this* bread and wine with the whole action of God in creation and redemption. The invocation of the Spirit helps to root the prayer in the city as it echoes Isaiah in mentioning the effect of the good news on the poor, the broken-hearted, captives and prisoners.

Eucharistic Prayer B owes its origin to 'Original eucharistic prayer, Text 1', published by the Roman Catholic International Consultation on English in the Liturgy, but has been considerably changed. The unnecessary split invocation of the original has gone: it is a common feature of all four prayers that there is only one invocation of the Spirit. And the treatment of sacrifice in the memorial is quite different. But the vivid use of paradox which is one of the features of the original has been retained and is the explanation for such phrases as 'silent music' and 'these gifts which we bring before you from your own creation.' The use of triplets – a series of three seasonal or thematic insertions at different points in the prayer – is an innovation. They may be omitted, and the prayer is then quite short, if that is what is needed. But when the triplets are used, and especially if the response is repeated, the prayer has a length and richness of variable imagery which enables it to be used frequently without being repetitive.

Eucharistic Prayer C has a very clear trinitarian structure, with a series of single-line responses, one for each person of the Trinity plus one each for bread and wine. There is only one word which can be varied for seasonal or thematic reasons: 'risen' can become 'crucified', 'ascended', or some other adjective to describe our Lord.

Eucharistic Prayer D is very short, with a narrative which couples the bread and wine together in taking and thanking while retaining the separate words, 'This is my . . .'. The memorial and invocation are combined in a way which should satisfy the differing views within the Church. . . But the main feature of the prayer is the gap between the dialogue and the Sanctus, where the preface should be. This is to be supplied from one of the seventeen thanksgivings in the Resource Section. There is a range of biblical and historical thanksgivings there, some quite long (a long preface is desirable on occasions, and possible because the rest of the prayer is so short) and others short, with single line, repetitive responses for which the congregation will not need the words. Having some prayers which can be used without the congregation having to have books or leaflets in front of them is one of the requests from our consultations in UPAs. This helps to meet that need, especially as in this prayer (as in Prayer B), the Sanctus, acclamations and doxology are the standard Rite A ones, in the traditional order.

CONCLUSION

The three parts of *Patterns for Worship* – the service outlines and samples, the resource sections, and the commentary – might be thought of as skeletons, or the bare bones and outlines of services, flesh to clothe them with, in terms of the resource material, and the working instructions or hints on how to make it all work. But like Ezekiel's army in the valley of dry bones, the skeletons need not only flesh and instructions, but the breath of the Lord himself, to bring them to life. So we offer to the Church dry bones, flesh and words, knowing that our brothers and sisters who lead the Church's worship will pray with us for the breath of God's Spirit to fill his people as they find a door open in heaven.

2 OUTLINE SERVICES AND INSTRUCTIONS

1 FORM OF SERVICE FOR MORNING OR EVENING PRAYER: THE SERVICE OF THE WORD

NOTE All variations of this form of service, and all forms used as part of it, shall be neither contrary to, nor indicative of any departure from, the doctrine of the Church of England in any essential matter. Appendix 2 amplifies this further, and Appendix 1 contains the legal information about introducing this form of service.

1 Introduction

There may be some singing, an introduction, scripture sentence, greeting or opening prayer.

2 Penitence

The minister may introduce the *confession*, using ASB Morning and Evening Prayer sections 3, 4, 26, 27, or Rite A Holy Communion sections 5, 6, 25, 26, or Resource Section 2 in *PatternsforWorship*, or other suitable words.

The form of *confession* and *absolution* must be one already authorized, or one from Resource Section 2 in *Patterns for Worship*.

3 Praise

Some responses must be used, either ones already authorized or from Resource Section 6 in *Patterns for Worship*.

Songs of praise are usually sung before the psalm and after each reading. Any of those in the ASB or in Resource Sections 62, 63, 65 or 66 may be used, but care should be taken to ensure that the traditional songs for Morning and Evening Prayer are sometimes used.

Other songs and hymns of praise may also be used.

4 The Word

This should normally include

- the *psalms* in some form, said or sung.
- *two (or possibly one) readings*, one from the Old Testament and one from the New Testament
- a *sermon*, either after one of the readings or before the prayers.
- on Sundays, an authorized version of one of the *Creeds*, or one of the Affirmations of Faith from Resource Section 4.

5 Prayers

These prayers of intercession may be in any suitable form, provided that at some point in the service

(a) the Lord's Prayer is said in an authorized form, and

(b) the collect of the day is used, with one of the collects from Section 22 in ASB Morning Prayer or Resource Section 52.

6 Ending

The service may end with any authorized form of blessing, one of the Endings on p.107 of the ASB or one from from Resource Section 9.

NOTE The order of sections 2-5 in this service may be varied as necessary.

2 FORM OF SERVICE FOR THE HOLY COMMUNION, RITE C

NOTE All variations of this form of service, and all forms used as part of it shall be neither contrary to, nor indicative of any departure from, the doctrine of the Church of England in any essential matter.

Part 1

This may consist of Sections 1-29 of Rite A Holy Communion or Morning or Evening Prayer or

The Service of the Word, as above, or as follows:

1 Preparation

There may be some singing, an introduction, scripture sentence, greeting or opening prayer.

Penitence must be used here or in Section 3.
The minister may introduce the *confession*, using ASB Morning and Evening Prayer sections 3, 4, 26, 27, or Rite A Holy Communion sections 5, 6, 25, 26, or Resource Section 2 in *Patterns for Worship*, or other suitable words.

The form of *confession* and *absolution* must be one already authorized, or one from Resource Section 2 in *Patterns for Worship*.

Kyrie, *Gloria*, or another song may be used.

The president says the *collect* - the prayer for the day.

2 The Word

Either two or three Bible *readings* (one of which shall be from the Gospel), psalms or songs.

Sermon

One of the *creeds* from the ASB or an Affirmation of Faith from Resource Section 4 must be used on Sundays.

3 The Prayers

The prayers of intercession may be in any suitable form.

All may say

We do not presume...

or the alternative prayer from ASB Holy Communion Rite A, section 82.

PART 2: THE HOLY COMMUNION

4 The preparation

The *PEACE* may come here. Any suitable introductory words may be used, ending with

The peace of the Lord be always with you
and also with you.

The *Preparation of the Gifts* may follow.

5 The Eucharistic Prayer

One of the authorized forms from the ASB or from Resource Section 8 must be used. All begin with this dialogue:

The Lord be with you **and also with you.**	*or*	The Lord is here. **His Spirit is with us.**

Lift up your hearts.
We lift them to the Lord.

Let us give thanks to the Lord our God.
It is right to give him thanks and praise.

The following abbreviation in printed texts is allowed in the case of the Eucharistic Prayers in the ASB and Eucharistic Prayer D from Resource Section 8; otherwise, the full Eucharistic Prayer must be reproduced.

The President leads the Thanksgiving for the work of Christ, ending

. . . for ever praising you and saying
Holy, holy, holy Lord,
God of power and might,
heaven and earth are full of your glory.
Hosanna in the highest.

This anthem may also be used

Blessed is he who comes in the name of the Lord,
Hosanna in the highest.

The words of Christ at the supper end

. . . in remembrance of me.

These acclamations, or ones from Resource Section 8, follow:

Christ has died;
Christ is risen;
Christ will come again.

The Eucharistic Prayer may end with

Amen.

or **Blessing and honour and glory and power**
be yours for ever and ever. Amen.

6 Breaking Bread and Sharing in Communion

The Lord's Prayer

The breaking of bread may be done in silence, or with the words at Section 43 in Rite A Holy Communion, or with one of the forms in the Resource Section 7.

The president invites the people to receive communion.
Each communicant replies **Amen** to the words of distribution.

7 After Communion

Post-communion prayer: Prayers from Rite A Sections 52, 53 or 86, or from Resource Section 52, or other suitable prayers are said.

The blessing and dismissal: The president may use any of the blessings provided in Rite A Sections 54 and 77, or in Resource Section 9. The dismissal should be in the form provided in Rite A Section 55.

3 INSTRUCTIONS FOR THE SERVICE OF THE WORD

This may be a service on its own or lead into the Holy Communion.
There should be a balance between four main ingredients:

Word
Prayer
Praise
Action

Order

These may be put in any order. Some logical progression, or development in the congregation's relationship to God should be reflected in the order. So, for example, the order might be

- Bible reading, followed by silence leading into
- prayer and praise, based on the reading.
- some action symbolizing going out in obedience to that word.

These ingredients may come more than once in the service. For example, in the outline above, there might be a hymn of praise before the readings.

How it works

FIRST, decide on the structure.

SECOND, 'clothe' the structure/skeleton with items from the Resource Sections (or from the Alternative Service Book, other resource books or from the work of a parish worship preparation group). So, for example, taking the structure above:

Word: Follow the Lectionary - or select one of the alternative routes.

If occasion demands, there need only be one reading.

The psalms should normally be used in some form.

If this service is the first part of the Holy Communion, one of the readings must be the Gospel.

There should normally be a sermon, which need not take a traditional form. There may be more than one person taking part, the congregation may divide into groups for all or part of the time, or the sermon may come in a number of parts at different points in the service. There should normally be some time for silent reflection after the readings or sermon.

Prayer: Look at the forms of prayer and decide whether to have

- an outline form filled in by the minister
- an outline form with extempore prayer or biddings from the congregation, or from a group
- a litany
- a series of set prayers.

It is best not to mix the forms too much, though a set prayer may be a good way to end or sum up one of the other forms. The Lord's Prayer and the collect for the day should be used at every Sunday service. If the prayers of penitence are used, there should be an authorized form of confession and forgiveness.

Praise – may be said or sung. Select hymns, songs, or items from the Praise pages of the Resource Section.

One of the sets of versicles and responses should normally be used.

Action This is not of the same order as the other three, and may be done at the same time as one of them. For example, dramatic action might interpret the word, or a procession or dance might help to express praise. Other actions might be

- a movement by the congregation, such as standing or joining hands
- movement with an object, e.g. candle or Bible
- a change in lighting or visual presentation

The action may be the climax to which the service moves, or an action that begins the worship and sets the theme for it.

THIRD, decide what other material you want to add.

You will need an introduction or preparation section, and an ending.

You may need to add creed, notices, collection, invitations or biddings, explanation, silence.

Decide how these ingredients relate to the aim and structure of the rest of the service. For example, prayers of penitence might be part of the preparation, at the beginning, to clear away any barrier to hearing God, or could be the climax to which the service moves (as in an Ash Wednesday service).

The full structure might then look like this:

(NOTE In all the examples that follow, an asterisk indicates material that *must* be used. A double asterisk indicates that only a limited number of texts is authorized.)

EXAMPLE 1 A block structure

Items you must include (though individual items and order will vary)			*Additional items you may want to add*
	1→	**Preparation**	Scripture sentence
	2→		Hymn
	3→		Opening prayer
	4→		Invitation
	5→		★★Confession
	6→		★★Forgiveness
Word	7→	Introduction	
★Old Testament	←8		
★Psalm or paraphrase	←9		
★New Testament	←10		
	11→	Song or hymn	
Talk	←12		
	13→	Hymn	
Prayer ★★Collect	←14		
★Form of intercession	←15		
Praise ★Versicles and responses	←16		
	17→	Hymn	
Action All stand while the candle is	←18		
carried out	19→	Blessing	

EXAMPLE 2 The conversation structure

Word - Prayer - Praise - Action may come many times within the same service. Imagine a conversation between God and the congregation. The **Word** items present what God is saying, and the other three items may be used as the response or reply to God. The service may be built from a series of **Presentation** and **Response** units, like building blocks. This example is from Morning Prayer:

PRESENTATION			RESPONSE	
Word	Scripture sentence	←1		
		2→	**Praise**	Hymn of adoration
Word	Invitation	←3		
		4→	**Prayer**	★★Confession
Prayer	★★Declaration of forgiveness	←5		
		6→	**Praise**	★Open our lips . . . Glory be . . .
		7→		Song
Word	★Psalm	←8		
	★Old Testament	←9		
		10→	**Praise**	Song
Word	★New Testament	←11		
		12→	**Praise**	Song
		13→	★★Creed	
		14→	★★Lord's Prayer	
		15→	★★Collect	
Word	Sermon	←16		
		17→	Hymn	

Themes

A theme may determine the pattern of the worship. The traditional Morning and Evening prayer pattern allows the word and praise to throw light on each other. A thematic approach means very often that the worship leader decides the way the word is to be heard, and the response that needs to be made. Care must be taken to make sure that the whole service does not become a sermon, with explanations and exhortations introducing every item.

Examples of a thematic approach would be Maundy Thursday foot-washing, Baptism service, Wisdom lays her table (Proverbs 9).

Guidelines

When you have completed the service outline, consider this checklist. Parts of this are amplified in the descriptive commentary in section 5.

1 Is there a balance between word, prayer, praise and action? For instance the Word section may be top heavy with long readings and long introductions, or too many short readings.

2 Is the worship directed to God, addressing him rather than the people?

3 Is the Word Service moving towards communion? If so, it must include an authorized form of penitence, a Gospel reading and (on Sundays) the creed.

4 What space is there for reflection or silence in the service?

5 How much of the service might be classed as 'entertainment'? Is this justified? Is there a balance between receiving (listening, watching, contemplating) and responding? Check on posture: is there too much sitting down or standing up at one time? Is there enough action?

6 Is the structure and direction of the service clear enough for people to know where it is going? Does the service have an overall coherence, or is it just one entertainment item after another?

7 Is the music used in such a way as to further and develop the main thrust of the service? Is there too much musical praise, with too many choir items, or too long a section of choruses from the band, or hymns too close to one another?

8 Does the service enable the gifts of a variety of people in the church to be used in both planning and taking part?

9 Compare this service with other services in the month. An occasional completely new form of worship may stimulate people to discover new dimensions to their ordinary worship, but a new pattern each week may be confusing and unsettling, particularly to children. If people are familiar with both structure and content of the service, they feel more secure and can take part more easily. For a family service, for instance, it may be better to have a standard structure, with 'windows' or 'slots' which can be changed from week to week.

10 Especially if you are planning family worship, check that the contents are not divisive, and can be used by children, single people, the bereaved, members of broken families. It is hurtful and not constructive to require a mixed congregation to join in prayers thanking God for our homes and families and all the happiness that parents and children share.

4 INSTRUCTIONS FOR THE EUCHARIST

This service is made up of two parts, the Word and the Sacrament. The Word Service consists of

Morning or Evening Prayer or

the first part of the Eucharist or

one of the Word Service patterns above.

The Sacrament consists of

Penitence (if it does not come in the Service of the Word)

The Peace

Preparation of the gifts

Eucharistic Prayer

Breaking of the bread

Communion

Conclusion

These features are not all of equal weight.

How it works

FIRST, decide on your structure.
For *Introduction*, *Word*, *Intercession* and *Penitence*, see previous section XXX.

SECOND, decide on those ingredients which are normal but may vary in position, i.e. where penitence is to come, and where the Peace is shared. (The text is printed before the preparation of the gifts, but it can come at other stages, for example at the end of the service.)

THIRD, decide on those ingredients in the service which are not compulsory; e.g. the collect for purity, the Gloria in excelsis, the prayer of humble access, the choice of post-communion prayers.

FOURTH, decide on those parts of the service where 'ad lib' or unofficial material may be used, or where there is provision made in the Resource Section, e.g. the introduction to the service, the introduction to the Peace, prayers at the presentation of the gifts, seasonal prayers after communion, responsive prayers, the alternative affirmations of faith.

The Peace Most modern rites place the Peace between the Prayers and the Preparation of the gifts. Note the scope for placing it elsewhere, as well as the option to introduce it with other words, which may be composed for the occasion or the locality.

Preparation of the Gifts Customs vary on the solemnity with which this is done. In some places, variable prayers may be used. These should be *preparatory*, as the title for this part implies, and not dramatically overshadow the eucharistic prayer. (See the Commentary, page XXX.)

Eucharistic Prayer One of the existing forms or permitted alternatives must always be used. A eucharistic prayer, whether it takes the form of extended monologue with acclamations, or a dialogue between president and congregation, normally includes the following:

– thanksgiving for creation, redemption and the work of the Spirit
– the memorial prayer for the church to receive and grow in the life of Christ
– doxology, offering praise to God the Holy Trinity.

These are the 'deep structures' of the prayer and they need to be clear in the shape of the ideas expressed within them - including the tone of voice(s) used as it is proclaimed.

This means that the pattern of the prayer is normally

an opening dialogue
an introduction to praise
an extended act of thanksgiving
the narrative of the institution
the memorial prayer
the prayer for the blessing of the Spirit
and the concluding doxology

But variations are permitted within this framework as follows:

– the proper preface: any of the prefaces in the Alternative Service Book or in Resource Section 64 may be used, provided that it balances with the style and overall length of the rest of the prayer.
– acclamations: the customary 'Christ has died' may be replaced by any of those listed under acclamations in Resource Section 8.

chorus or metrical versions of the Sanctus and Doxology may be used, instead of those printed.

The Eucharistic Prayer leads into the Lord's Prayer.

Breaking of the Bread
This symbolic action prepares for the sharing of the bread and wine. It may be done in silence or one of the forms in the ASB or the Resource Section may be used.

Invitation to Communion
There are forms for this at sections 45 and 85 of Rite A Holy Communion.

Communion
Local customs vary. However the bread and wine are shared, it should be done decently and in order. Bread and wine not required for communion is reverently consumed at the end of the distribution or after the service. This is not a significant liturgical act and need not be done at the holy table or by the president.

After Communion
Variable prayers after communion, or responsive prayers, may be used at this point. Other alternative prayers and dismissals are provided in the Resource Section.

3 SAMPLE SERVICES

suggested for publication as cards

NOTES

1 The sample services that follow provide examples of how the outlines and instructions work, using material from the ASB and the Resource Sections. They are not intended as 'ideal' services designed by the Commission for everyone to use, though the intention is that a good number of them will be provided as service cards, with bold headings and illustrations.[1] It is for this reason that there is considerable variety both in the range of seasonal and standard services offered, and in the variety of headings and rubrics.

2 Words to be said by the congregation are in **bold** type.

---

[1]Examples of the service cards envisaged by the Commission are provided in GS Misc 328, available from Church House Bookshop, 31 Great Smith Street, London SW1P 3BN.

Hear his voice today

INTRODUCTION

Singing, introduction, scripture sentence, greeting or prayer

The PEACE may be exchanged after the introductory words

The peace of the Lord be always with you:
and also with you.

This is the day which the Lord has made:
Let us rejoice and be glad in it.

**Lord, direct our thoughts,
teach us to pray,
lift up our hearts to worship you
in Spirit and in truth,
through Jesus Christ. Amen.**

WE CONFESS OUR SINS

Either

**Lord God,
we have done evil in your sight;
we have sinned against you alone.
We are sorry and repent.
Have mercy on us according to your love.
Wash away our wrong-doing and cleanse us from our sin.
Renew a right spirit within us
and restore us to the joy of your salvation,
through Jesus Christ our Lord. Amen.**

Lord, we are clay,
and you are the potter.
We are all the work of your hand.
Do not remember our sins for ever.

Look upon us in your mercy:
for we are your people.

or

Almighty God, our heavenly Father,
we have sinned against you and against
our neighbour,
in thought and word and deed,
through negligence, through weakness,
through our own deliberate fault.
We are truly sorry,
and repent of all our sins.
For the sake of your Son Jesus Christ,
who died for us,
forgive us all that is past;
and grant that we may serve you in newness of life
to the glory of your name. Amen.

The minister declares God's forgiveness.

PRAISE

O Lord, open our lips:
and our mouth shall proclaim your praise.

Let us worship the Lord:
All praise to his name.

Glory to the Father, and to the Son,
and to the Holy Spirit:
as it was in the beginning, is now,
and shall be for ever. Amen.

Psalm or song

THE WORD

Psalms or songs

Either one or two readings
At the end of each the reader may say

This is the word of the Lord:
Thanks be to God.

Sermon

THE APOSTLES' CREED

Do you believe and trust in God the Father,
who made all things?

**I believe in God, the Father almighty,
creator of heaven and earth.**

Do you believe and trust in his Son Jesus Christ,
who redeemed the world?

**I believe in Jesus Christ, his only Son, our Lord.
He was conceived by the power of the Holy Spirit
and born of the Virgin Mary.
He suffered under Pontius Pilate,
was crucified, died, and was buried.
He descended to the dead.
On the third day he rose again.
He ascended to heaven,
and is seated at the right hand of the Father.
He will come again to judge the living
and the dead.**

Do you believe and trust in the Holy Spirit,
who gives life to the people of God?

**I believe in the Holy Spirit,
the holy catholic Church,
the communion of saints,
the forgiveness of sins,
the resurrection of the body
and the life everlasting. Amen.**

PRAYERS

The prayers may include some of these responses

Lord, have mercy upon us.
Christ, have mercy upon us.
Lord, have mercy upon us.

or Lord, in your mercy
hear our prayer

or Jesus, Lord of . . .
in your mercy, hear us.

and end with

Merciful Father:
accept these prayers
for the sake of your Son,
our Saviour Jesus Christ. Amen.

Our Father in heaven,
hallowed be your name,
your kingdom come,
your will be done,
on earth as in heaven.
Give us today our daily bread.
Forgive us our sins
as we forgive those who sin against us.
Lead us not into temptation
but deliver us from evil.

For the kingdom, the power, and the glory are yours
now and for ever. Amen.

Collect

God of power,
may the boldness of your Spirit transform us,
may the gentleness of your Spirit lead us,
may the gifts of your Spirit
equip us to serve and worship you,
now and always. Amen.

2 GENERAL: WITH EVENING OPTIONS

The Service of the Word

INTRODUCTION

A Song or hymn

We have come together as the family of God
in our Father's presence
to offer him praise and thanksgiving,
to hear and receive his holy word,
to bring before him the needs of the world,
to ask his forgiveness of our sins,
and to seek his grace,
that through his Son Jesus Christ
we may give ourselves to his service.

or

O Lord, we call to you: come to us quickly:
Hear us when we cry to you.

Let our prayer be set forth in your sight as incense:
The lifting up of our hands as the evening sacrifice.

We confess our sins

God is light.
In God there is no darkness.
If we live in the light,
as God is in the light,
we have fellowship with one another,
and the blood of Jesus, his Son, purifies us from all sin.

**Almighty God, our heavenly Father,
we have sinned against you and against
our neighbour,
in thought and word and deed,
through negligence, through weakness,
through our own deliberate fault.
We are truly sorry,
and repent of all our sins.**

For the sake of your Son Jesus Christ,
who died for us,
forgive us all that is past;
and grant that we may serve you in newness of life
to the glory of your name. Amen.

The minister declares God's forgiveness.

THE WORD

Collect

Psalms or songs

Either one or two readings
At the end of each the reader may say

This is the word of the Lord:
Thanks be to God.

Sermon

THE APOSTLES' CREED

I believe in God, the Father almighty,
creator of heaven and earth.

I believe in Jesus Christ, his only Son, our Lord.
He was conceived by the power of the Holy Spirit
and born of the Virgin Mary.
He suffered under Pontius Pilate,
was crucified, died, and was buried.
He descended to the dead.
On the third day he rose again.
He ascended to heaven,
and is seated at the right hand of the Father.
He will come again to judge the living and the dead.

I believe in the Holy Spirit,
the holy catholic Church
the communion of saints,
the forgiveness of sins,
the resurrection of the body
and the life everlasting. Amen.

PRAISE

O Lord, open our lips:
and our mouth shall proclaim your praise.

Let us worship the Lord:
All praise to his name.

Glory to the Father, and to the Son,
and to the Holy Spirit:
as it was in the beginning, is now,
and shall be for ever. Amen.

Psalm or song

PRAYERS

The prayers may include some of these responses

Lord, have mercy upon us.
Christ, have mercy upon us.
Lord, have mercy upon us.

or Lord in your mercy
hear our prayer

or Jesus, Lord of . . .
in your mercy, hear us.

and end with

Merciful Father:
accept these prayers
for the sake of your Son,
our Saviour Jesus Christ. Amen.

or this form may be used

(We pray to the Lord, saying
'In faith we pray:
We pray to you our God.')

That the rest of this day may be holy, peaceful and full of your presence.
In faith we pray:
We pray to you our God.

That the work we have done and the people we have met today may bring us closer to you.
In faith we pray:
We pray to you our God.

That we may hear and respond to your call to peace and justice.
In faith we pray:
We pray to you our God.

That you will sustain the faith and hope of those who are lonely, oppressed and anxious.
In faith we pray:
We pray to you our God.

That you will strengthen us in your service,
and fill our hearts with longing for your kingdom,
In faith we pray:
We pray to you our God.

God our Saviour,
You know us and love us
and hear our prayer:
keep us in the eternal fellowship
of Jesus Christ our Saviour. Amen.

Our Father in heaven,
hallowed be your name,
your kingdom come,
your will be done,
on earth as in heaven.
Give us today our daily bread.
Forgive us our sins
as we forgive those who sin against us.
Lead us not into temptation
but deliver us from evil.

For the kingdom, the power, and the glory
are yours
now and for ever. Amen.

ENDING

Gracious God, you have given us much today;
grant us also a thankful spirit.
Into your hands we commend ourselves
and those we love.
Stay with us, and when we take our rest
renew us for the service of your Son Jesus Christ. **Amen.**

**In darkness and in light,
in trouble and in joy,
help us heavenly Father,
to trust your love,
to serve your purpose,
and to praise your name,
through Jesus Christ our Lord. Amen.**

Jesus Christ is the light of the world:
the light no darkness can overcome.

Stay with us, Lord, for it is evening:
and the day is almost over.

Let your light scatter the darkness:
and shine through your Church.

You, Christ, are the King of glory:
you are the everlasting Son of the Father.

When you drew the sting of death:
you opened heaven to all who trust in you.

Come then, we pray, to the aid of your people:
we are bought at the price of your own precious blood.

When you make up the number of your saints:
reward us with them in glory for ever. Amen.

Mercy, peace and love be ours for ever:
from God the Father, Son and Holy Spirit. Amen.

The Peace

Sovereign Lord, your word has been fulfilled;
my eyes have seen your salvation:
now you let your servant go in peace.

The peace of the Lord be always with you:
and also with you.

Christ is our peace

The Holy Communion

We say together the lines in bold type

WE PREPARE

Singing, greeting and prayer, which may include

The Lord be with you
and also with you.

**Almighty God,
to whom all hearts are open,
all desires known,
and from whom no secrets are hidden:
cleanse the thoughts of our hearts
by the inspiration of your Holy Spirit,
that we may perfectly love you,
and worthily magnify your holy name;
through Christ our Lord. Amen.**

WE CONFESS

**Almighty God, our heavenly Father,
we have sinned against you and against
our neighbour,
in thought and word and deed,
through negligence, through weakness,
through our own deliberate fault.
We are truly sorry,
and repent of all our sins.
For the sake of your Son Jesus Christ,
who died for us,
forgive us all that is past;
and grant that we may serve you in newness of life
to the glory of your name. Amen.**

The president declares God's forgiveness.

WE PRAISE

This song may be said or sung.

**Glory to God in the highest,
and peace to his people on earth.**

**Lord God, heavenly King,
almighty God and Father,
we worship you, we give you thanks,
we praise you for your glory.**

**Lord Jesus Christ, only Son of the Father,
Lord God, Lamb of God,
you take away the sin of the world:
have mercy on us;
you are seated at the right hand of the Father:
receive our prayer.**

**For you alone are the Holy One,
you alone are the Lord,
you alone are the Most High,
Jesus Christ,
with the Holy Spirit,
in the glory of God the Father. Amen.**

The president says the Collect - the prayer for the day.

WE LISTEN TO GOD'S WORD

*Either two or three readings follow.
At the end of the reading the reader may say*

This is the word of the Lord.
Thanks be to God.

Before the Gospel **Glory to Christ our Saviour.**
and at the end **Praise to Christ our Lord.**

*There may be psalms or songs.
Sermon, talk or instruction*

THE APOSTLES' CREED

**I believe in God, the Father almighty,
creator of heaven and earth.**

**I believe in Jesus Christ, his only Son, our Lord.
He was conceived by the power of the Holy Spirit
and born of the Virgin Mary.
He suffered under Pontius Pilate,
was crucified, died, and was buried.
He descended to the dead.
On the third day he rose again.
He ascended to heaven,
and is seated at the right hand of the Father.
He will come again to judge the living
and the dead.**

**I believe in the Holy Spirit,
the holy catholic Church,
the communion of saints,
the forgiveness of sins,
the resurrection of the body
and the life everlasting. Amen.**

WE PRAY

The prayers sometimes include the response

Lord in your mercy
Hear our prayer.

and end with

**Merciful Father,
accept these prayers
for the sake of your Son,
our Saviour Jesus Christ. Amen.**

We sometimes say

**We do not presume
to come to this your table, merciful Lord,
trusting in our own righteousness,
but in your manifold and great mercies.
We are not worthy
so much as to gather up the crumbs under
your table.**

But you are the same Lord
whose nature is always to have mercy.
Grant us therefore, gracious Lord,
so to eat the flesh of your dear Son
Jesus Christ
and to drink his blood,
that we may evermore dwell in him
and he in us. Amen.

The Peace

After the introductory words

The peace of the Lord be always with you
and also with you.

WE GIVE THANKS IN THE EUCHARISTIC PRAYER

The Lord be with you
and also with you.

or

The Lord is here.
His Spirit is with us.

Lift up your hearts.
We lift them to the Lord.

Let us give thanks to the Lord our God.
It is right to give him thanks and praise.

The President leads the Thanksgiving for the work of Christ, ending

. . . for ever praising you and saying:

Holy, holy, holy Lord,
God of power and might,
heaven and earth are full of your glory.
Hosanna in the highest.

This anthem may also be used.

Blessed is he who comes in the name of the Lord.
Hosanna in the highest.

The words of Christ at the supper end
. . . in remembrance of me.

Christ has died;
Christ is risen;
Christ will come again.

The Eucharistic Prayer may end with

Amen.

or **Blessing and honour and glory and power
be yours for ever and ever. Amen.**

WE BREAK BREAD AND SHARE IN COMMUNION

As our Saviour taught us, so we pray
**Our Father in heaven,
hallowed be your name,
your kingdom come,
your will be done,
on earth as in heaven.
Give us today our daily bread.
Forgive us our sins
as we forgive those who sin against us.
Lead us not into temptation
but deliver us from evil.**

**For the kingdom, the power, and the glory
are yours
now and for ever. Amen.**

We break this bread
to share in the body of Christ.
**Though we are many, we are one body,
because we all share in one bread.**

*The president invites the people to receive communion.
Each communicant replies* **Amen** *to the words of distribution.*

AFTER COMMUNION

**Almighty God,
We thank you for feeding us
with the body and blood of your Son
Jesus Christ.
Through him we offer you our souls and bodies
to be a living sacrifice.
Send us out in the power of your Spirit
to live and work
to your praise and glory. Amen.**

THE DISMISSAL

The blessing may be said.

Go in peace to love and serve the Lord.
In the name of Christ. Amen.

or Go in the peace of Christ.
Thanks be to God.

Holy Communion

PREPARATION

Singing, greeting and prayer

The president says the Collect - the prayer for the day

Kyrie eleison may be said

Lord, have mercy.
Lord, have mercy.

Christ, have mercy.
Christ, have mercy.

Lord, have mercy.
Lord, have mercy.

THE MINISTRY OF THE WORD

Either two or three readings follow.
At the end of the reading the reader may say

This is the word of the Lord.
Thanks be to God.

Before the Gospel	**Glory to Christ our Saviour.**
and at the end	**Praise to Christ our Lord.**

There may be psalms or songs.
Sermon, talk or instruction

THE NICENE CREED

We believe in one God,
the Father, the almighty,
maker of heaven and earth,
of all that is, seen and unseen.

We believe in one Lord, Jesus Christ,
the only Son of God,
eternally begotten of the Father,
God from God, Light from Light,
true God from true God,

**begotten, not made,
of one Being with the Father.
Through him all things were made.
For us men and for our our salvation
he came down from heaven;
by the power of the Holy Spirit
he became incarnate of the Virgin Mary,
and was made man.
For our sake he was crucified under
Pontius Pilate;
he suffered death and was buried.
On the third day he rose again,
in accordance with the Scriptures;
He ascended into heaven
and is seated at the right hand of the Father.
He will come again in glory
to judge the living and the dead,
and his kingdom will have no end.**

**We believe in the Holy Spirit,
the Lord, the giver of life,
who proceeds from the Father and the Son.
With the Father and the Son he is worshipped
and glorified.
He has spoken through the Prophets.**

**We believe in one holy catholic
and apostolic Church.
We acknowledge one baptism for the
forgiveness of sins.
We look for the resurrection of the dead,
and the life of the world to come. Amen.**

PRAYERS

The prayers sometimes include the response

Lord in your mercy
Hear our prayer.

and end with

Merciful Father,
**accept these prayers
for the sake of your Son,
our Saviour Jesus Christ. Amen.**

PENITENCE

The Commandments or the Summary of the Law may be used, with the response

Amen. Lord, have mercy.

**Almighty God, our heavenly Father,
we have sinned against you,
through our own fault,
in thought and word and deed,
and in what we have left undone.
For your Son our Lord Jesus Christ's sake,
forgive us all that is past;
and grant that we may serve you in newness of life
to the glory of your name. Amen.**

The president declares God's forgiveness.

All may say

**We do not presume
to come to this your table, merciful Lord,
trusting in our own righteousness,
but in your manifold and great mercies.
We are not worthy
so much as to gather up the crumbs under
your table.
But you are the same Lord
whose nature is always to have mercy.
Grant us therefore, gracious Lord,
so to eat the flesh of your dear Son
Jesus Christ
and to drink his blood,
that we may evermore dwell in him
and he in us. Amen.**

The Peace may come here. Any suitable introductory words may be used, ending with

The peace of the Lord be always with you
and also with you.

After the gifts have been prepared, the president says

THE EUCHARISTIC PRAYER

The Lord be with you *or* The Lord is here.
and also with you. **His Spirit is with us.**

Lift up your hearts.
We lift them to the Lord.

Let us give thanks to the Lord our God.
It is right to give him thanks and praise.

The President leads the Thanksgiving for the work of Christ, ending

. . . for ever praising you and saying:

Holy, holy, holy Lord,
God of power and might,
heaven and earth are full of your glory.
Hosanna in the highest.

This anthem may also be used.

Blessed is he who comes in the name of the Lord.
Hosanna in the highest.

The words of Christ at the supper end

. . . in remembrance of me.

Christ has died;
Christ is risen;
Christ will come again.

The Eucharistic Prayer ends with

Amen.

or **Blessing and honour and glory and power**
be yours for ever and ever. Amen.

BREAKING BREAD AND SHARING IN COMMUNION

As our Saviour taught us, so we pray
Our Father in heaven,
hallowed be your name,
your kingdom come,
your will be done,
on earth as in heaven.
Give us today our daily bread.
Forgive us our sins
as we forgive those who sin against us.

Lead us not into temptation
but deliver us from evil.

For the kingdom, the power, and the glory
are yours
now and for ever. Amen.

The breaking of bread may be done in silence, or with one of the forms in the Resource Section (73), or with these words

We break this bread
to share in the body of Christ.
Though we are many, we are one body,
because we all share in one bread.

Either here or later we may sing

Lamb of God, you take away the sins of the world:
have mercy on us.

Lamb of God, you take away the sins of the world:
have mercy on us.

Lamb of God, you take away the sins of the world:
grant us peace.

The president invites the people to receive communion.
Each communicant replies **Amen** *to the words of distribution.*

AFTER COMMUNION

Almighty God,
We thank you for feeding us
with the body and blood of your Son
Jesus Christ.
Through him we offer you our souls and bodies
to be a living sacrifice.
Send us out in the power of your Spirit
to live and work
to your praise and glory. Amen.

THE DISMISSAL

The blessing may be said.

Go in peace to love and serve the Lord.
In the name of Christ. Amen.

or Go in the peace of Christ.
Thanks be to God.

5 GENERAL

Holy Communion

WE PREPARE

Singing, greeting and prayer, which may include

The Lord be with you
and also with you.

**Almighty God,
to whom all hearts are open,
all desires known,
and from whom no secrets are hidden:
cleanse the thoughts of our hearts
by the inspiration of your Holy Spirit,
that we may perfectly love you,
and worthily magnify your holy name;
through Christ our Lord. Amen.**

WE CONFESS

**Father eternal, giver of light and grace,
we have sinned against you and against our neighbour,
in what we have thought,
in what we have said and done,
through ignorance, through weakness,
through our own deliberate fault.**

**We have wounded your love,
and marred your image in us.
We are sorry and ashamed,
and repent of all our sins.**

**For the sake of your Son Jesus Christ, who died for us,
forgive us all that is past;
and lead us out from darkness
to walk as children of light. Amen.**

The president declares God's forgiveness.

WE PRAISE

This song may be said or sung

**Glory to God in the highest,
and peace to his people on earth.**

**Lord God, heavenly King,
almighty God and Father,
we worship you, we give you thanks,
we praise you for your glory.**

**Lord Jesus Christ, only Son of the Father,
Lord God, Lamb of God,
you take away the sin of the world:
have mercy on us;
you are seated at the right hand of the Father:
receive our prayer.**

**For you alone are the Holy One,
you alone are the Lord,
you alone are the Most High,
Jesus Christ,
with the Holy Spirit,
in the glory of God the Father. Amen.**

The president says the Collect - the prayer for the day.

WE LISTEN TO GOD'S WORD

*Either two or three readings follow.
At the end of the reading the reader may say*

This is the word of the Lord.
Thanks be to God.

Before the Gospel	**Glory to Christ our Saviour.**
and at the end	**Praise to Christ our Lord.**

*There may be psalms or songs.
Sermon, talk or instruction*

WE BELIEVE

Do you believe and trust in God the Father,
who made all things?

I believe and trust in him.

Do you believe and trust in his Son Jesus Christ,
who redeemed the world?

I believe and trust in him.

Do you believe and trust in his Holy Spirit,
who gives life to the people of God?

I believe and trust in him.

This is the faith of the Church.
This is our faith.
We believe and trust in one God,
Father, Son, and Holy Spirit.

WE PRAY

The prayers may include the response

Lord in your mercy
Hear our prayer.

and end with

Merciful Father,
accept these prayers
for the sake of your Son,
our Saviour Jesus Christ. Amen.

All may say

Most merciful Lord,
your love compels us to come in.
Our hands were unclean
our hearts were unprepared;
we were not fit
even to eat the crumbs from under your table.
But you, Lord, are the God of our salvation,
and share your bread with sinners.
So cleanse us and feed us
with the precious body and blood of your Son,
that he may live in us and we in him;
and that we, with the whole company of Christ,
may sit and eat in your kingdom. Amen.

The Peace

After the introductory words

The peace of the Lord be always with you
and also with you.

WE GIVE THANKS IN THE EUCHARISTIC PRAYER

The Lord be with you *or* The Lord is here.
and also with you. **His Spirit is with us.**

Lift up your hearts.
We lift them to the Lord.

Let us give thanks to the Lord our God.
It is right to give him thanks and praise.

The President leads the Thanksgiving for the work of Christ, ending

. . . for ever praising you and saying

Holy, holy, holy Lord,
God of power and might,
heaven and earth are full of your glory.
Hosanna in the highest.

This anthem may also be used.

Blessed is he who comes in the name of the Lord.
Hosanna in the highest.

The words of Christ at the supper end

. . . in remembrance of me.

We proclaim the mystery of faith.
Christ has died;
Christ is risen;
Christ will come again.

The Eucharistic Prayer ends with

Amen.

or **Blessing and honour and glory and power**
be yours for ever and ever. Amen.

WE BREAK BREAD AND SHARE IN COMMUNION

As our Saviour taught us, so we pray
Our Father in heaven,
hallowed be your name,
your kingdom come,
your will be done,
on earth as in heaven.
Give us today our daily bread.
Forgive us our sins
as we forgive those who sin against us.
Lead us not into temptation
but deliver us from evil.

For the kingdom, the power, and the glory
are yours
now and for ever. Amen.

The breaking of bread may be done in silence, or with one of the forms in the Resource Section (73), or with these words

Every time we eat this bread and drink this cup
we proclaim the Lord's death until he comes.

The president invites the people to receive communion.

Jesus is the Lamb of God
who takes away the sin of the world.
Happy are those who are called to his supper.
Lord, I am not worthy to receive you,
but only say the word, and I shall be healed.

Each communicant replies **Amen** *to the words of distribution.*

AFTER COMMUNION

Almighty God,
We thank you for feeding us
with the body and blood of your Son
Jesus Christ.
Through him we offer you our souls and bodies
to be a living sacrifice.
Send us out in the power of your Spirit
to live and work
to your praise and glory. Amen.

THE DISMISSAL

The blessing may be said.

Go in peace to love and serve the Lord.
In the name of Christ. Amen.

or Go in the peace of Christ.
Thanks be to God.

The Lord is here

The Eucharist

WE PREPARE

Singing, greeting and prayer, which may include

This is the day which the Lord has made.
Let us rejoice and be glad in it.

**Lord, direct our thoughts,
teach us to pray,
lift up our hearts to worship you
in Spirit and in truth,
through Jesus Christ. Amen.**

or

**Almighty God,
to whom all hearts are open,
all desires known,
and from whom no secrets are hidden:
cleanse the thoughts of our hearts
by the inspiration of your Holy Spirit,
that we may perfectly love you,
and worthily magnify your holy name;
through Christ our Lord. Amen.**

Let us return to the Lord our God and say to him

**Father,
we have sinned against heaven and against you.
We are not worthy to be called your children.
We turn to you again.
Have mercy on us,
bring us back to yourself
as those who once were dead
but now have life through Christ our Lord. Amen.**

May God our Father forgive us our sins,
and bring us to the fellowship of his table
with his saints for ever. **Amen.**

WE PRAISE

This or a similar song may be sung

**Glory to God, glory to God,
Glory to the Father.
To him be glory for ever
Alleluia ! Amen.**

**Glory to God, glory to God,
Son of the Father,
To him be glory for ever
Alleluia ! Amen.**

**Glory to God, glory to God,
Glory Holy Spirit.
To him be glory for ever
Alleluia ! Amen.**

The president says the Collect - the prayer for the day.

THE MINISTRY OF THE WORD

Either two or three readings follow.
At the end of the reading the reader may say

This is the word of the Lord.
Thanks be to God.

Before the Gospel	**Glory to Christ our Saviour.**
and at the end	**Praise to Christ our Lord.**

There may be psalms or songs.
Sermon, talk or instruction

Do you believe and trust in God the Father,
who made all things?

We believe and trust in him.

Do you believe and trust in his Son Jesus Christ,
who redeemed the world?

We believe and trust in him.

Do you believe and trust in his Holy Spirit,
who gives life to the people of God?

We believe and trust in him.

This is the faith of the Church
This is our faith.
We believe and trust in one God:
Father, Son and Holy Spirit. Amen.

WE PRAY

The prayers sometimes include the response

Lord in your mercy
Hear our prayer

and end with

Merciful Father,
accept these prayers
for the sake of your Son,
our Saviour Jesus Christ. Amen.

We stand for the Peace.

After the introductory words

The peace of the Lord be always with you
and also with you.

After the gifts have been prepared, the president says

THE EUCHARISTIC PRAYER

The Lord be with you *or* The Lord is here.
and also with you. **His Spirit is with us.**

Lift up your hearts.
We lift them to the Lord.

Let us give thanks to the Lord our God.
It is right to give him thanks and praise.

For the Preface, a Thanksgiving from Patterns for Worship *is used.*

Father, we give you thanks and praise
through Jesus Christ your Son, our Lord,
because. . .

We may join in

We worship and adore you.

It ends
So, with angels and archangels, and all the company of heaven,
we praise you for ever, saying

Holy, holy, holy Lord,
God of power and might,
heaven and earth are full of your glory.
Hosanna in the highest.

We sometimes say

Blessed is he who comes in the name of the Lord.

Hosanna in the highest.

Praise and thanks to you, Father in heaven:
on the night before he died
your Son Jesus Christ took bread and wine.
He gave thanks and said
This is my body, given for you.
This is my blood, shed for the forgiveness of sins.

Christ has died:
Christ is risen:
Christ will come again.

Pour out your Holy Spirit
as we bring before you these gifts
and remember his sacrifice
made once for all on the cross.
Feed us with his body and blood,
that we may live and grow in him.

Through him we worship you, Father almighty,
in songs of everlasting praise:

Blessing and honour and glory and power
be yours for ever and ever. Amen.

Silence should be kept.

The Lord's Prayer is said either as follows or in its traditional form.

As our Saviour taught us, so we pray
Our Father in heaven,
hallowed be your name,

your kingdom come,
your will be done,
on earth as in heaven.
Give us today our daily bread.
Forgive us our sins
as we forgive those who sin against us.
Lead us not into temptation
but deliver us from evil.

For the kingdom, the power, and the glory
are yours
now and for ever. Amen.

The president breaks the consecrated bread, either in silence or saying this or another authorized form.

We break this bread
to share in the body of Christ.
Though we are many, we are one body,
because we all share in one bread.

The President invites the people to receive communion.
Each communicant replies **Amen** *to the words of distribution.*

AFTER COMMUNION

Almighty God,
we thank you for feeding us
with the body and blood of your Son
Jesus Christ.
Through him we offer you our souls and bodies
to be a living sacrifice.
Send us out in the power of your Spirit
to live and work
to your praise and glory. Amen.

THE DISMISSAL

The blessing may be said

Go in peace to love and serve the Lord.
In the name of Christ. Amen.

or Go in the peace of Christ
Thanks be to God.

ADVENT

Holy Communion

PREPARATION

Singing, greeting and prayer, which may include

We hear what sounds like a large crowd,
like the sound of a roaring waterfall,
like loud peals of thunder:
Praise God! For the Lord, our Almighty God, is King!
Happy are those who have been invited
to the wedding-feast of the Lamb.
Alleluia !

We confess our sins

Almighty God, our heavenly Father,
we have sinned against you and against
our neighbour,
in thought and word and deed,
through negligence, through weakness,
through our own deliberate fault.
We are truly sorry,
and repent of all our sins.
For the sake of your Son Jesus Christ,
who died for us,
forgive us all that is past;
and grant that we may serve you in newness
of life
to the glory of your name. Amen.

The president declares God's forgiveness.

The president says the Collect - the prayer for the day.

THE MINISTRY OF THE WORD

At the end of the reading the reader may say

This is the word of the Lord.
Thanks be to God.

Before the Gospel **Glory to Christ our Saviour.**
and at the end **Praise to Christ our Lord.**

We have two or three readings, psalms or songs.
Sermon, talk or instruction

We say together in faith

Holy, holy, holy
is the Lord God Almighty,
who was, and is, and is to come.

We believe in God the Father,
who created all things:
for by his will they were created
and have their being.

We believe in God the Son,
who was slain:
for with his blood,
he purchased us for God,
from every tribe and language,
from every people and nation.

We believe in God the Holy Spirit –
the Spirit and the Bride say, 'Come !'
Even so, come Lord Jesus ! Amen.

PRAYERS

In joyful expectation of his coming to our aid
we pray to Jesus, saying

Maranatha
Come, Lord Jesus.

Come to your Church as Lord and Judge.
We pray for . . .
Help us to live in the light of your coming
and give us a longing for your rule.
Maranatha
Come, Lord Jesus.

Come to your world as King of the nations.
We pray for . . .
Before you rulers will stand in silence.
Maranatha
Come, Lord Jesus.

Come to your people with a message of victory and peace.
We pray for . . .
Give us the victory over death, temptation and evil.
Maranatha
Come, Lord Jesus.

Come to us as Saviour and Comforter.
We pray for . . .
Break in to those areas of our lives
where we live with failure and distress,
and set us free to serve you for ever.
Maranatha
Come, Lord Jesus.

Come to us from heaven with power and great glory,
to lift us up to meet you,
with all your saints and angels,
to live with you for ever.
Maranatha
Come, Lord Jesus.

We stand for the Peace.

The God of peace makes us holy in all things
that we may be ready at the coming of our Lord Jesus Christ.

The peace of the Lord be always with you
and also with you.

After the gifts have been prepared, the president says

THE EUCHARISTIC PRAYER

The Lord be with you **and also with you.**	*or*	The Lord is here. **His Spirit is with us.**

Lift up your hearts.
We lift them to the Lord.

Let us give thanks to the Lord our God.
It is right to give him thanks and praise.

The President leads the Thanksgiving for the work of Christ, ending

. . . for ever praising you and saying

**Holy, holy, holy Lord,
God of power and might,
heaven and earth are full of your glory.
Hosanna in the highest.**

This anthem may also be used.

**Blessed is he who comes in the name of the Lord.
Hosanna in the highest.**

The words of Christ at the supper end

. . . in remembrance of me.

**Christ has died;
Christ is risen;
Christ will come again.**

The Eucharistic Prayer ends with

Amen.

or **Blessing and honour and glory and power
be yours for ever and ever. Amen.**

BREAKING BREAD AND SHARING IN COMMUNION

We pray for the coming of the kingdom
in the words our Saviour taught us.

**Our Father in heaven,
hallowed be your name,
your kingdom come,
your will be done,
on earth as in heaven.
Give us today our daily bread.
Forgive us our sins
as we forgive those who sin against us.
Lead us not into temptation
but deliver us from evil.**

**For the kingdom, the power, and the glory
are yours
now and for ever. Amen.**

The breaking of bread may be done in silence, or with these or similar words

God of promise,
you prepare a banquet for us in your kingdom.
Happy are those who are called
to the supper of the Lamb.

The President invites the people to receive communion.
Each communicant replies **Amen** *to the words of distribution.*

AFTER COMMUNION

Generous God,
you have fed us at your heavenly table.
Kindle us with the fire of your Spirit
that at the coming of Christ
we may shine like lights before his face;
who lives and reigns with you and the Holy Spirit
in glory for ever. Amen.

or

Almighty God,
We thank you for feeding us
with the body and blood of your Son
Jesus Christ.
Through him we offer you our souls and bodies
to be a living sacrifice.
Send us out in the power of your Spirit
to live and work
to your praise and glory. Amen.

The blessing

Go in peace to love and serve the Lord.
In the name of Christ. Amen.

Peace to his people on earth

Holy Communion at Christmas

PREPARATION

Singing, greeting and prayers, which may include

The Word was made flesh and lived among us:
and we have seen his glory.

This song may be said or sung.

**Glory to God in the highest,
and peace to his people on earth.**

**Lord God, heavenly King,
almighty God and Father,
we worship you, we give you thanks,
we praise you for your glory.**

**Lord Jesus Christ, only Son of the Father,
Lord God, Lamb of God,
you take away the sin of the world:
have mercy on us;
you are seated at the right hand of the Father:
receive our prayer.**

**For you alone are the Holy One,
you alone are the Lord,
you alone are the Most High,
Jesus Christ,
with the Holy Spirit,
in the glory of God the Father. Amen.**

THE MINISTRY OF THE WORD

The president says the Collect - the prayer for the day.

At the end of the reading the reader may say

This is the word of the Lord.
Thanks be to God.

Before the Gospel	**Glory to Christ our Saviour.**
and at the end	**Praise to Christ our Lord.**

We have two or three readings, psalms or songs.
Sermon, talk or instruction

We proclaim the Church's faith in Jesus Christ.

We believe and declare that our Lord Jesus Christ,
the Son of God, is both divine and human;

God, of the being of the Father,
the only Son from before time began;
human from the being of his mother, born in the world.

Fully God and fully human;
one human person with mind and body.

As God he is equal to the Father,
as human he is less than the Father.

Although he is both divine and human
he is not two beings but one Christ.

One, not by turning God into flesh,
but by taking humanity into God.

Truly one, not by having a hybrid nature,
but by being one person.

For as mind and body form one human being
so the one Christ is both divine and human.

The Word became flesh and lived among us;
we have seen his glory,
the glory of the only Son from the Father,
full of grace and truth.

PRAYERS

These may include the response

Lord in your mercy
Hear our prayer.

God our Saviour:
You know us and love us
and hear our prayer:
keep us in the eternal fellowship
of Jesus Christ our Saviour. Amen.

CONFESSION

The light of the world has come into the world and pierces the darkness of our hearts. In that light let us examine ourselves and confess our sins.

Silence should be kept.

Lord of grace and truth,
we confess our unworthiness
to stand in your presence as your children.
We have sinned:
forgive – and heal us.

The Virgin Mary accepted your call
to be the mother of Jesus.
Forgive our disobedience to your will.
We have sinned:
forgive – and heal us.

Your Son our Saviour
was born in poverty in a manger.
Forgive our greed and rejection of your ways.
We have sinned:
forgive – and heal us.

The shepherds left their flocks
to go to Bethlehem.
Forgive our self-interest and lack of vision.
We have sinned:
forgive – and heal us.

The wise men followed the star
to find Jesus the King.
Forgive our reluctance to seek you.
We have sinned:
forgive – and heal us.

May the God of all healing and forgiveness
draw you to himself,
that you may behold the glory of his Son,
the Word made flesh,
and be cleansed from all your sins
through Jesus Christ our Lord. **Amen.**

We stand for the Peace

Glory to God in the highest,
and on earth peace to all on whom his favour rests:
The peace of the Lord be always with you
and also with you. Alleluia !

After the gifts have been prepared, the president says

THE EUCHARISTIC PRAYER

The Lord be with you
and also with you.

or

The Lord is here.
His Spirit is with us.

Lift up your hearts.
We lift them to the Lord.

Let us give thanks to the Lord our God.
It is right to give him thanks and praise.

The President leads the Thanksgiving for the work of Christ, ending

. . . for ever praising you and saying

Holy, holy, holy Lord,
God of power and might,
heaven and earth are full of your glory.
Hosanna in the highest.

This anthem may also be used.

Blessed is he who comes in the name of the Lord.
Hosanna in the highest.

The words of Christ at the supper end

. . . in remembrance of me.

Christ has died;
Christ is risen;
Christ will come again.

The Eucharistic Prayer ends with

Amen.

or **Blessing and honour and glory and power**
be yours for ever and ever. Amen.

BREAKING BREAD AND SHARING IN COMMUNION

As our Saviour taught us, so we pray
Our Father in heaven,
hallowed be your name,
your kingdom come,
your will be done,
on earth as in heaven.
Give us today our daily bread.
Forgive us our sins
as we forgive those who sin against us.
Lead us not into temptation
but deliver us from evil.

For the kingdom, the power, and the glory
are yours
now and for ever. Amen.

The breaking of bread may be done in silence, or with one of the forms in the Resource Section (73), or with these words

We break the bread of life
and that life is the light of the world:
God here among us,
light in the midst of us,
bring us to light and life.

The President invites the people to receive communion.
Each communicant replies **Amen** *to the words of distribution.*

AFTER COMMUNION

Almighty God,
We thank you for feeding us
with the body and blood of your Son
Jesus Christ.
Through him we offer you our souls and bodies
to be a living sacrifice.
Send us out in the power of your Spirit
to live and work
to your praise and glory. Amen.

The blessing

Go in peace to love and serve the Lord.
In the name of Christ. Amen.

LENT

Holy Communion

PREPARATION

Singing, greeting and prayer, which may include

Jesus is the Lamb of God:
who takes away the sins of the world.

Almighty God,
to whom all hearts are open,
all desires known,
and from whom no secrets are hidden:
cleanse the thoughts of our hearts
by the inspiration of your Holy Spirit,
that we may perfectly love you,
and worthily magnify your holy name;
through Christ our Lord. Amen.

We call to mind our sin and God's promise of forgiveness.

Cast your burden upon the Lord:
And he will sustain you.
Create in us clean hearts, O God:
And renew a right spirit within us.
Cast us not away from your presence:
And take not your Holy Spirit from us.
Give us the joy of your saving help again:
And sustain us with your life-giving Spirit.

Lord God,
we have done evil in your sight;
we have sinned against you alone.
We are sorry and repent.
Have mercy on us according to your unfailing love.
Wash away all our wrong-doing and cleanse us from our sin.
Renew a right spirit within us
and restore us to the joy of your salvation,
through Jesus Christ our Lord. Amen.

May the God of forgiveness
show *us* his mercy,
forgive *us our* sins,
and bring *us* to everlasting life,
through Jesus Christ our Lord. **Amen.**

Kyrie eleison may be said.

Lord, have mercy.
Lord, have mercy.

Christ, have mercy.
Christ, have mercy.

Lord, have mercy.
Lord, have mercy.

The president says the Collect - the prayer for the day.

THE MINISTRY OF THE WORD

Either two or three readings follow.
At the end of the reading the reader may say

This is the word of the Lord.
Thanks be to God.

Before the Gospel **Glory to Christ our Saviour.**
and at the end **Praise to Christ our Lord.**

There may be psalms or songs.
Sermon, talk or instruction

Let us affirm our faith in Jesus Christ the Son of God.

Though he was divine,
he did not cling to equality with God,
but made himself nothing.
Taking the form of a slave,
he was born in human likeness.
As a man he humbled himself,
and was obedient to death –
even the death of the cross.
Therefore God has raised him on high,
and given him the name above every name:
that at the name of Jesus

every knee should bow,
and every voice proclaim
that Jesus Christ is Lord,
to the glory of God the Father. Amen.

PRAYERS

These may include the response

Lord in your mercy
Hear our prayer.

and end with

Merciful Father,
accept these prayers
for the sake of your Son,
our Saviour Jesus Christ. Amen.

All may say

We do not presume
to come to this your table, merciful Lord,
trusting in our own righteousness,
but in your manifold and great mercies.
We are not worthy
so much as to gather up the crumbs under your table.
But you are the same Lord
whose nature is always to have mercy.
Grant us therefore, gracious Lord,
so to eat the flesh of your dear Son Jesus Christ
and to drink his blood,
that we may evermore dwell in him
and he in us. Amen.

We stand for the Peace

Now that we have been put right with God through faith,
we have peace with God through our Lord Jesus Christ:
The peace of the Lord be always with you
and also with you.

After the gifts have been prepared, the president says

THE EUCHARISTIC PRAYER

The Lord be with you *or* The Lord is here.
and also with you. **His Spirit is with us.**

Lift up your hearts.
We lift them to the Lord.

Let us give thanks to the Lord our God.
It is right to give him thanks and praise.

The President leads the Thanksgiving for the work of Christ, ending

. . . for ever praising you and saying

Holy, holy, holy Lord,
God of power and might,
heaven and earth are full of your glory.
Hosanna in the highest.

This anthem may also be used.

Blessed is he who comes in the name of the Lord,
Hosanna in the highest.

The words of Christ at the supper end

. . . in remembrance of me.

Christ has died;
Christ is risen;
Christ will come again.

The Eucharistic Prayer ends with

Amen.

or **Blessing and honour and glory and power**
be yours for ever and ever. Amen.

BREAKING BREAD AND SHARING IN COMMUNION

As our Saviour taught us, so we pray
Our Father in heaven,
hallowed be your name,
your kingdom come,
your will be done,
on earth as in heaven.
Give us today our daily bread.

Forgive us our sins
as we forgive those who sin against us.
Lead us not into temptation
but deliver us from evil.

For the kingdom, the power, and the glory
are yours
now and for ever. Amen.

The breaking of bread may be done in silence, or with these or similar words

Every time we eat this bread
and drink this cup:
we proclaim the Lord's death
until he comes.

The president invites the people to receive communion.
Each communicant replies **Amen** *to the words of distribution.*

AFTER COMMUNION

Merciful God,
you have called us to your table
and fed us with the bread of life.
Draw us and all people to your Son,
our Saviour Jesus Christ.

or

Almighty God,
We thank you for feeding us
with the body and blood of your Son
Jesus Christ.
Through him we offer you our souls and bodies
to be a living sacrifice.
Send us out in the power of your Spirit
to live and work
to your praise and glory. Amen.

You believe God will not despise
a broken spirit and a contrite heart:
Amen.

You believe Christ bore your sins
in his body on the tree;
you have been healed by his wounds:
Amen.
May he give you a spirit of repentance day by day,
pardon, peace, and the assurance of sins forgiven:
Amen.
and the blessing . . .

Go in the peace of Christ.
Thanks be to God.

EASTER

Holy Communion

PREPARATION

Singing, greeting and prayer, which may include

Alleluia ! Christ is risen.
He is risen indeed. Alleluia !

Jesus is the resurrection and the life. Alleluia !
Those who believe in him shall never die. Alleluia !

Almighty God,
to whom all hearts are open,
all desires known,
and from whom no secrets are hidden:
cleanse the thoughts of our hearts
by the inspiration of your Holy Spirit,
that we may perfectly love you,
and worthily magnify your holy name;
through Christ our Lord. Amen.

We confess our sins

Almighty God, our heavenly Father,
we have sinned against you and against our neighbour,
in thought and word and deed,
through negligence, through weakness,
through our own deliberate fault.
We are truly sorry,
and repent of all our sins.
For the sake of your Son Jesus Christ,
who died for us,
forgive us all that is past;
and grant that we may serve you in newness of life
to the glory of your name. Amen.

The president declares God's forgiveness.

This song may be said or sung.

**Glory to God in the highest,
and peace to his people on earth.**

**Lord God, heavenly King,
almighty God and Father,
we worship you, we give you thanks,
we praise you for your glory.**

**Lord Jesus Christ, only Son of the Father,
Lord God, Lamb of God,
you take away the sin of the world:
have mercy on us;
you are seated at the right hand of the Father:
receive our prayer.**

**For you alone are the Holy One,
you alone are the Lord,
you alone are the Most High,
Jesus Christ,
with the Holy Spirit,
in the glory of God the Father. Amen.**

THE MINISTRY OF THE WORD

The president says the Collect - the prayer for the day.

*Either two or three readings follow.
At the end of the reading the reader may say*

This is the word of the Lord.
Thanks be to God.

Before the Gospel **Glory to Christ our Saviour.**
and at the end **Praise to Christ our Lord.**

or

Alleluial ! Christ is risen:
The Lord is risen indeed. Alleluia !

Praise the God and Father of our Lord Jesus Christ:
**He gave us new life and hope!
He has raised Jesus from the dead!**

God has claimed us as his own:
He has brought us out of darkness!
He has made us lights to the world!

Alleluia ! Christ is risen:
He is risen indeed. Alleluia !

There may be psalms or songs.
Sermon, talk or instruction

THE NICENE CREED

We believe in one God,
the Father, the almighty,
maker of heaven and earth,
of all that is, seen and unseen.

We believe in one Lord, Jesus Christ,
the only Son of God,
eternally begotten of the Father,
God from God, Light from Light,
true God from true God,
begotten, not made,
of one Being with the Father.
Through him all things were made.
For us men and for our our salvation
he came down from heaven;
by the power of the Holy Spirit
he became incarnate of the Virgin Mary,
and was made man.
For our sake he was crucified under
Pontius Pilate;
he suffered death and was buried.
On the third day he rose again,
in accordance with the Scriptures;
He ascended into heaven
and is seated at the right hand of the Father.
He will come again in glory
to judge the living and the dead,
and his kingdom will have no end.

We believe in the Holy Spirit,
the Lord, the giver of life,
who proceeds from the Father and the Son.

With the Father and the Son he is worshipped and glorified.
He has spoken through the Prophets.

We believe in one holy catholic and apostolic Church.
We acknowledge one baptism for the forgiveness of sins.
We look for the resurrection of the dead,
and the life of the world to come. Amen.

PRAYERS

These may include the response

Lord, hear us.
Lord, graciously hear us.

or

Lord in your mercy
Hear our prayer.

and end with

Merciful Father,
accept these prayers
for the sake of your Son,
our Saviour Jesus Christ. Amen.

All may say

We do not presume
to come to this your table, merciful Lord,
trusting in our own righteousness,
but in your manifold and great mercies.
We are not worthy
so much as to gather up the crumbs under your table.
But you are the same Lord
whose nature is always to have mercy.
Grant us therefore, gracious Lord,
so to eat the flesh of your dear Son Jesus Christ
and to drink his blood,
that we may evermore dwell in him
and he in us. Amen.

We stand for the Peace

The introductory words end

Alleluia ! The peace of the risen Christ be always with you
and also with you. Alleluia !

After the gifts have been prepared, the president says

THE EUCHARISTIC PRAYER

The Lord be with you
and also with you.

or

The Lord is here.
His Spirit is with us.

Lift up your hearts.
We lift them to the Lord.

Let us give thanks to the Lord our God.
It is right to give him thanks and praise.

The President leads the Thanksgiving for the work of Christ, ending

. . . for ever praising you and saying

Holy, holy, holy Lord,
God of power and might,
heaven and earth are full of your glory.
Hosanna in the highest.

This anthem may also be used.

Blessed is he who comes in the name of the Lord.
Hosanna in the highest.

The words of Christ at the supper end

. . . in remembrance of me.

Christ has died;
Christ is risen;
Christ will come again.

The Eucharistic Prayer ends with

Amen.

or **Blessing and honour and glory and power**
be yours for ever and ever. Amen.

BREAKING BREAD AND SHARING IN COMMUNION

As our Saviour taught us, so we pray
Our Father in heaven,
hallowed be your name,
your kingdom come,
your will be done,
on earth as in heaven.
Give us today our daily bread.
Forgive us our sins
as we forgive those who sin against us.
Lead us not into temptation
but deliver us from evil.

For the kingdom, the power, and the glory
are yours
now and for ever. Amen.

The breaking of bread may be done in silence, or with one of the forms in the Resource Section (73), or with these words

We break this bread
to share in the body of Christ.
Though we are many, we are one body,
because we all share in one bread.

The president invites the people to receive communion, ending with these words

Alleluia ! Christ our Passover is sacrificed for us.
Alleluia ! Let us keep the feast.

Each communicant replies **Amen** *to the words of distribution.*

AFTER COMMUNION

God of truth,
we have seen with our eyes
and touched with our hands
the bread of life.
Strengthen our faith
that we may grow in love for you
and for each other;
through Jesus Christ our risen Lord. Amen.

or

**Father of all,
we give you thanks and praise,
that when we were still far off
you met us in your Son and brought us home.
Dying and living, he declared your love,
gave us grace,
and opened the gate of glory.
May we who share Christ's body
live his risen life;
we who drink his cup
bring life to others;
we whom the Spirit lights
give light to the world.
Keep us firm in the hope you have set before us,
so we and all your children shall be free,
and the whole earth live to praise your name;
through Christ our Lord. Amen.**

The blessing

Go in peace to love and serve the Lord.
  Alleluia ! Alleluia !
In the name of Christ. Alleluia ! Alleluia !

PENTECOST

Holy Communion

PREPARATION

Singing, greeting and prayer, which may include

This is the day which the Lord has made. Alleluia !
Let us rejoice and be glad in it. Alleluia!

God has given us his spirit.
He has poured out his love.

Almighty God,
to whom all hearts are open,
all desires known,
and from whom no secrets are hidden:
cleanse the thoughts of our hearts
by the inspiration of your Holy Spirit,
that we may perfectly love you,
and worthily magnify your holy name;
through Christ our Lord. Amen.

We confess our sins

Almighty God, our heavenly Father,
we have sinned against you and against our neighbour,
in thought and word and deed,
through negligence, through weakness,
through our own deliberate fault.
We are truly sorry,
and repent of all our sins.
For the sake of your Son Jesus Christ, who died for us,
forgive us all that is past;
and grant that we may serve you in newness of life
to the glory of your name. Amen.

The president declares God's forgiveness.

This song may be said or sung.

**Glory to God in the highest,
and peace to his people on earth.**

**Lord God, heavenly King,
almighty God and Father,
we worship you, we give you thanks,
we praise you for your glory.**

**Lord Jesus Christ, only Son of the Father,
Lord God, Lamb of God,
you take away the sin of the world:
have mercy on us;
you are seated at the right hand of the Father:
receive our prayer.**

**For you alone are the Holy One,
you alone are the Lord,
you alone are the Most High,
Jesus Christ, with the Holy Spirit,
in the glory of God the Father. Amen.**

The president says the Collect - the prayer for the day.

THE MINISTRY OF THE WORD

*Either two or three readings follow
At the end of the reading the reader may say*

This is the word of the Lord.
Thanks be to God.

Before the Gospel **Glory to Christ our Saviour.**
and at the end **Praise to Christ our Lord.**

*There may be psalms or songs.
Sermon, talk or instruction*

THE NICENE CREED

We believe in one God,
the Father, the almighty:

**maker of heaven and earth,
of all that is, seen and unseen.**

We believe in one Lord, Jesus Christ,
the only Son of God,
eternally begotten of the Father:

God from God, Light from Light,
true God from true God,

begotten, not made
of one Being with the Father:

through him all things were made.

For us men and for our salvation
he came down from heaven;
by the power of the Holy Spirit
he became incarnate of the Virgin Mary,
and was made man.

For our sake he was crucified under
Pontius Pilate;
he suffered death and was buried.

On the third day he rose again
in accordance with the Scriptures:

he ascended into heaven
and is seated at the right hand of the Father.
He will come again in glory
to judge the living and the dead,
and his kingdom will have no end.

We believe in the Holy Spirit:

the Lord, the giver of life,

who proceeds from the Father and the Son:

with the Father and the Son he is worshipped
and glorified.

He has spoken through the Prophets.

We believe in one holy, catholic and apostolic Church.

We acknowledge one baptism for the forgiveness of sins.

We look for the resurrection of the dead,
and the life of the world to come. Amen.

PRAYERS

These may include the response

Lord in your mercy.
Hear our prayer.

and end with

Lord of the Church:
Hear our prayer,
and make us one in heart and mind
to serve you in Christ our Lord. Amen.

All may say

We do not presume
to come to this your table, merciful Lord,
trusting in our own righteousness,
but in your manifold and great mercies.
We are not worthy
so much as to gather up the crumbs under your table.
But you are the same Lord
whose nature is always to have mercy.
Grant us therefore, gracious Lord,
so to eat the flesh of your dear Son Jesus Christ
and to drink his blood,
that we may evermore dwell in him
and he in us. Amen.

We stand for the Peace

The fruit of the Spirit is love, joy, peace.
If we live in the Spirit, let us walk in the Spirit.
The peace of the Lord be always with you
and also with you. Alleluia!

After the gifts have been prepared, the president says

THE EUCHARISTIC PRAYER

The Lord be with you
and also with you.

or

The Lord is here.
His Spirit is with us.

Lift up your hearts.
We lift them to the Lord.

Let us give thanks to the Lord our God.
It is right to give him thanks and praise.

The President leads the Thanksgiving for the work of Christ, ending

. . . for ever praising you and saying

Holy, holy, holy Lord,
God of power and might,
heaven and earth are full of your glory.
Hosanna in the highest.

This anthem may also be used.

Blessed is he who comes in the name of the Lord.
Hosanna in the highest.

The words of Christ at the supper end

. . . in remembrance of me.

Christ has died;
Christ is risen;
Christ will come again.

The Eucharistic Prayer ends with

Amen.

or **Blessing and honour and glory and power**
be yours for ever and ever. Amen.

BREAKING BREAD AND SHARING IN COMMUNION

As our Saviour taught us, so we pray
Our Father in heaven,
hallowed be your name,
your kingdom come,
your will be done,
on earth as in heaven.
Give us today our daily bread.
Forgive us our sins
as we forgive those who sin against us.
Lead us not into temptation
but deliver us from evil.

For the kingdom, the power, and the glory
are yours
now and for ever. Amen.

The breaking of bread may be done in silence, or with one of the forms in the Resource Section (73), or with these words

We break this bread
to share in the body of Christ.
Though we are many, we are one body,
because we all share in one bread.

The president invites the people to receive communion.
Each communicant replies **Amen** *to the words of distribution.*

AFTER COMMUNION

God of power,
may the boldness of your Spirit transform us,
may the gentleness of your Spirit lead us,
may the gifts of your Spirit
equip us to serve and worship you
now and always. Amen.

or

Almighty God,
We thank you for feeding us
with the body and blood of your Son
Jesus Christ.
Through him we offer you our souls and bodies
to be a living sacrifice.
Send us out in the power of your Spirit
to live and work
to your praise and glory. Amen.

The blessing

Jesus said, 'Receive the Spirit:
as the Father sent me, so I send you.'

Go in peace to love and serve the Lord.
Alleluia ! Alleluia !
In the name of Christ. Alleluia ! Alleluia !

All Creation Worships

Holy Communion

PREPARATION

Singing, greeting and prayer, which may include

Great is the Lord and worthy of all praise:
**Amen ! Praise and glory and wisdom,
thanksgiving and honour, power and might,
be to our God for ever and ever ! Amen. (Alleluia !)**

**Almighty God,
to whom all hearts are open,
all desires known,
and from whom no secrets are hidden:
cleanse the thoughts of our hearts
by the inspiration of your Holy Spirit,
that we may perfectly love you,
and worthily magnify your holy name;
through Christ our Lord. Amen.**

*We confess our sins, and the sins of our society,
in the misuse of God's creation.*

God our Father, we are sorry
that we have often used your gifts carelessly,
and acted as though we were not grateful.
Hear our prayer, and in your mercy:
forgive us and help us.

We enjoy the fruits of the harvest,
but forget that you have given them to us.
Father, in your mercy:
forgive us and help us.

We are full and satisfied,
but ignore the cry of the hungry.
Father, in your mercy:
forgive and help us.

We are thoughtless,
and do not care for the world you have made.
Father, in your mercy:
forgive us and help us.

We store up goods for ourselves alone,
as if there were no God and no heaven.
Father, in your mercy:
forgive us and help us.

The Lord enrich *us* with his grace,
and nourish *us* with his blessing;
the Lord defend *us* in trouble and keep *us* from all evil;
the Lord accept *our* prayers,
and absolve *us* from *our* offences,
for the sake of Jesus Christ, our Saviour. **Amen.**

This song may be said or sung.

**Glory to God in the highest,
and peace to his people on earth.**

**Lord God, heavenly King,
almighty God and Father,
we worship you, we give you thanks,
we praise you for your glory.**

**Lord Jesus Christ, only Son of the Father,
Lord God, Lamb of God,
you take away the sin of the world:
have mercy on us;
you are seated at the right hand of the Father:
receive our prayer.**

**For you alone are the Holy One,
you alone are the Lord,
you alone are the Most High,
Jesus Christ,
with the Holy Spirit,
in the glory of God the Father. Amen.**

THE MINISTRY OF THE WORD

Either two or three readings
At the end of the reading the reader may say

This is the word of the Lord.
Thanks be to God.

Before the Gospel **Glory to Christ our Saviour.**
and at the end **Praise to Christ our Lord.**

There may be psalms or songs.
Sermon, talk or instruction

THE APOSTLES' CREED

Do you believe and trust in God the Father,
who made all things?

I believe in God, the Father almighty,
creator of heaven and earth.

Do you believe and trust in his Son Jesus Christ,
who redeemed the world?

I believe in Jesus Christ, his only Son, our Lord.
He was conceived by the power of the Holy Spirit
and born of the Virgin Mary.
He suffered under Pontius Pilate,
was crucified, died and was buried.
He descended to the dead.
On the third day he rose again.
He ascended into heaven,
and is seated at the right hand of the Father.
He will come again to judge the living and the dead.

Do you believe and trust in the Holy Spirit,
who gives life to the people of God?

I believe in the Holy Spirit,
the holy catholic Church,
the communion of saints,
the forgiveness of sins,
the resurrection of the body,
and the life everlasting.

This is the faith of the Church.
This is our faith.
We believe in one God,
Father, Son and Holy Spirit.

PRAYERS

These may include the response

Lord in your mercy
Hear our prayer.

and end with

Lord of creation, God our Saviour:
You know us and love us
and hear our prayer:
keep us in the eternal fellowship
of Jesus Christ our Saviour. Amen.

The president says the Collect - the prayer for the day.

All may say

We do not presume
to come to this your table, merciful Lord,
trusting in our own righteousness,
but in your manifold and great mercies.
We are not worthy
so much as to gather up the crumbs under your table.
But you are the same Lord
whose nature is always to have mercy.
Grant us therefore, gracious Lord,
so to eat the flesh of your dear Son Jesus Christ
and to drink his blood,
that we may evermore dwell in him
and he in us. Amen.

We stand for the Peace

Peacemakers who sow in peace raise a harvest of righteousness.
The peace of the Lord be always with you
and also with you. Alleluia !

After the gifts have been prepared, the president says

THE EUCHARISTIC PRAYER

The Lord be with you
and also with you.

or

The Lord is here.
His Spirit is with us.

Lift up your hearts.
We lift them to the Lord.

Let us give thanks to the Lord our God.
It is right to give him thanks and praise.

The President leads the Thanksgiving for the work of Christ, ending

. . . for ever praising you and saying

Holy, holy, holy Lord,
God of power and might,
heaven and earth are full of your glory.
Hosanna in the highest.

This anthem may also be used.

Blessed is he who comes in the name of the Lord.
Hosanna in the highest.

The words of Christ at the supper end

. . . in remembrance of me.

Christ has died;
Christ is risen;
Christ will come again.

The Eucharistic Prayer may end with

Amen.

or **Blessing and honour and glory and power**
be yours for ever and ever. Amen.

BREAKING BREAD AND SHARING IN COMMUNION

As our Saviour taught us, so we pray
Our Father in heaven,
hallowed be your name,
your kingdom come,
your will be done,
on earth as in heaven.
Give us today our daily bread.
Forgive us our sins
as we forgive those who sin against us.
Lead us not into temptation
but deliver us from evil.

For the kingdom, the power, and the glory
are yours
now and for ever. Amen.

The breaking of bread may be done in silence, or with one of the forms in the Resource Section (73), or with these words

Creator of all,
we have gathered many grains
and made them into this one bread:
We look for your Church to be gathered
from the ends of the earth
into the kingdom.

The president invites the people to receive communion.
Each communicant replies **Amen** *to the words of distribution.*

AFTER COMMUNION

Creator God,
you give seed for us to sow,
and bread for us to eat;
make us thankful for what we have received;
make us able to do those generous things
which supply your people's needs;
so all the world may give you thanks and glory.

Almighty God,
We thank you for feeding us
with the body and blood of your Son
Jesus Christ.
Through him we offer you our souls and bodies
to be a living sacrifice.
Send us out in the power of your Spirit
to live and work
to your praise and glory. Amen.

The blessing

Go in peace to love and serve the Lord.
In the name of Christ. Amen.

13 FOR A BAPTISM

Believe and trust

Holy Communion

PREPARATION

Singing, greeting and prayer, which may include

There is one body and one Spirit:
one Lord, one faith, one baptism.

We confess our sins

**God our Father,
long-suffering, full of grace and truth.
You create us from nothing and give us life.
You redeem us and make us your children by baptism.
You do not turn your face from us.
You do not cast us aside.
We confess that we have sinned against you
and our neighbour.
We have wounded your love
and marred your image in us.
For the sake of your Son,
restore us and bring us to your heavenly joy and peace,
in Jesus Christ our Lord. Amen.**

The president declares God's forgiveness.

This song may be said or sung.

**Glory to God in the highest,
and peace to his people on earth.**

**Lord God, heavenly King,
almighty God and Father,
we worship you, we give you thanks,
we praise you for your glory.**

**Lord Jesus Christ, only Son of the Father,
Lord God, Lamb of God,
you take away the sin of the world:**

**have mercy on us;
you are seated at the right hand of the Father:
receive our prayer.**

**For you alone are the Holy One,
you alone are the Lord,
you alone are the Most High,
Jesus Christ,
with the Holy Spirit,
in the glory of God the Father. Amen.**

The president says the Collect - the prayer for the day.

THE MINISTRY OF THE WORD

*Either two or three readings
At the end of the reading the reader may say*

This is the word of the Lord.
Thanks be to God.

Before the Gospel **Glory to Christ our Saviour.**
and at the end **Praise to Christ our Lord.**

*There may be psalms or songs.
Sermon, talk or instruction*

If children are to be baptized, the minister reads the duties of parents and godparents, who answer **I am willing.**

We thank God for our baptism to life in Christ, and we pray for *these children (N)* and say together

**Heavenly Father, in your love
you have called us to know you,
led us to trust you,
and bound our life with yours.
Surround *these children* with your love;
protect *them* from evil;
fill *them* with your Holy Spirit;
and receive *them* into the family of your Church;
that *they* may walk with us in the way of Christ
and grow in the knowledge of your love. Amen.**

THE DECISION

The minister asks

Do you turn to Christ?
I turn to Christ.

Do you repent of your sins?
I repent of my sins.

Do you renounce evil?
I renounce evil.

After the minister has made the sign of the cross on the forehead of those to be baptized

Do not be ashamed to confess the faith of Christ crucified.

Fight valiantly under the banner of Christ
against sin, the world, and the devil,
and continue his faithful *soldier* **and** *servant*
to the end of your *life.*

THE BAPTISM

Praise God who made heaven and earth,
who keeps his promise for ever.

After the prayer before the water of baptism the minister addresses the parents and godparents

Do you believe and trust in God the Father,
who made all things?
I believe and trust in him.

Do you believe and trust in his Son Jesus Christ,
who redeemed the world?
I believe and trust in him.

Do you believe and trust in his Holy Spirit,
who gives life to the people of God?
I believe and trust in him.

This is the faith of the Church.
This is our faith.
We believe and trust in one God,
Father, Son, and Holy Spirit.

The minister dips each one in the water or pours water on, saying

N, I baptize you in the name of the Father,
and of the Son, and of the Holy Spirit. **Amen.**

A lighted candle may be presented for each child.

Receive this light.

This is to show that you have passed
from darkness to light.
Shine as a light in the world
to the glory of God the Father.

PRAYERS

If children have been baptized. this prayer may be used here or at the end of the service.

Father in heaven,
bless these parents,
that they may love *their child.*
Make them wise and understanding,
to help *him/her* as *he/she* grows,
and surround *this family*
with the light of your truth
and the warmth of your love;
through Jesus Christ our Lord. Amen.

The intercessions may be in this form, or other suitable words may be used.

(We pray for God's grace, saying
Lord, receive our praise:
and hear our prayer.)

Lord God, through your grace we are your people:
through your Son you have redeemed us;
in your Spirit you have made us as your own.

We pray for . . . (new Christians, the Church . . .)
Make our hearts respond to your love.
Lord, receive our praise:
and hear our prayer.

We pray for . . . (the world, society, the local community)
Make our lives bear witness to your glory in the world.
Lord, receive our praise:
and hear our prayer.

We pray for . . . (people in need, Christian service)
Make our wills eager to obey, and our hands ready to heal.
Lord, receive our praise:
and hear our prayer.

We give thanks for . . .
Make our voices one with all your people in heaven and on earth.
Lord of the Church:
Hear our prayer,
and make us one in heart and mind
to serve you in Christ our Lord. Amen.

We stand for the Peace

The president says

God has received us by baptism into his Church.
We are members together of the body of Christ;
we are children of the same heavenly Father;
we are inheritors together of the kingdom of God.

The peace of the Lord be always with you
and also with you. Alleluia !

After the gifts have been prepared, the president says

THE EUCHARISTIC PRAYER

The Lord be with you **and also with you.**	*or*	The Lord is here. **His Spirit is with us.**

Lift up your hearts.
We lift them to the Lord.

Let us give thanks to the Lord our God.
It is right to give him thanks and praise.

The President leads the Thanksgiving for the work of Christ, ending

. . . for ever praising you and saying

Holy, holy, holy Lord,
God of power and might,
heaven and earth are full of your glory.
Hosanna in the highest.

This anthem may also be used.

Blessed is he who comes in the name of the Lord.
Hosanna in the highest.

The words of Christ at the supper end

. . . in remembrance of me.

Christ has died;
Christ is risen;
Christ will come again.

The Eucharistic Prayer ends with

Amen.

or **Blessing and honour and glory and power**
be yours for ever and ever. Amen.

BREAKING BREAD AND SHARING IN COMMUNION

As our Saviour taught us, so we pray
Our Father in heaven,
hallowed be your name,
your kingdom come,
your will be done,
on earth as in heaven.
Give us today our daily bread.
Forgive us our sins
as we forgive those who sin against us.
Lead us not into temptation
but deliver us from evil.
For the kingdom, the power, and the glory
are yours
now and for ever. Amen.

The breaking of bread may be done in silence, or with one of the forms in the Resource Section (73), or with these words

We break this bread
to share in the body of Christ.
Though we are many, we are one body,
because we all share in one bread.

The president invites the people to receive communion.
Each communicant replies **Amen** *to the words of distribution.*

AFTER COMMUNION

**Father, in baptism we die to sin,
rise again to new life
and find our true place in your living body.
May the new covenant sealed in Christ's blood
bring healing and reconciliation to this wounded world;
through Jesus Christ our Lord. Amen.**

or

**Almighty God,
We thank you for feeding us
with the body and blood of your Son
Jesus Christ.
Through him we offer you our souls and bodies
to be a living sacrifice.
Send us out in the power of your Spirit
to live and work
to your praise and glory. Amen.**

The Lord God almighty is our Father:
He loves us and cares tenderly for us.

The Lord Jesus Christ is our Saviour:
He has redeemed us and will defend us to the end.

The Lord, the Holy Spirit, is among us:
He will lead us in God's holy way.

**To God almighty, Father, Son and Holy Spirit,
be praise and glory today and for ever. Amen.**

Go in the peace of Christ:
Thanks be to God.

4 RESOURCE SECTIONS

CONTENTS OF THE RESOURCE SECTIONS

1 INTRODUCTIONS

The way a service begins can sometimes set the tone for all that follows: so it is important to prepare. Well-prepared notices, including some announcement of the day's theme, can serve to unite a congregation as a family with many concerns coming together for worship. The Peace may be used as an introduction. Rite A provides for a sentence of Scripture, a hymn, canticle or psalm (which might be an introit by choir alone, or a solo invitation to worship), and a greeting which the president may vary. Some ways of varying this greeting are indicated below. A prayer of preparation for worship might be used, similar in intention to that at section 3 in Rite A: some examples of this are given below, but must replace rather than be used alongside section 3. A spoken verse of a hymn might be used.
'Alleluia!' may be added at appropriate seasons to many of these introductions.

1 O Lord, we call to you: come to us quickly.
Hear us when we cry to you.

Let our prayer be set forth in your sight as incense,
The lifting up of our hands as the evening sacrifice.

Glory to the Father, and to the Son,
and to the Holy Spirit:
as it was in the beginning, is now,
and shall be for ever. Amen.
(Alleluia!) *Psalm 141.1,2*

2 Praise our God, all you his servants:
those who fear him, both small and great. *Revelation 19.5*

3 Grace and peace to you from God.
May he fill you with truth and joy.

4 This is the day which the Lord has made.
Let us rejoice and be glad in it. *Psalm 118.24*

5 **Lord, direct our thoughts,**
teach us to pray,
lift up our hearts to worship you
in Spirit and in truth,
through Jesus Christ. Amen.

6 We hear what sounds like a large crowd,
like the sound of a roaring waterfall,
like loud peals of thunder:
Praise God! For the Lord, our Almighty God, is King!
Happy are those who have been invited
to the wedding-feast of the Lamb.
(Alleluia!) *Revelation 19.6, 9*

7 **Loving Lord, fill us with your life-giving,**
joy-giving,
peace-giving presence
that we may praise you now with our lips
and all the day long with our lives;
through Jesus Christ our Lord. Amen.

8 *Reconciliation*
We stand before the throne of God
with countless crowds
from every nation and race, tribe and language:
Salvation belongs to our God!
(Alleluia!) *Revelation 7.9*

9 *City*
We have come to the city of the living God,
to the heavenly Jerusalem,
with thousands of angels in joyful assembly:
Alleluia!

We have come to God the judge of all,
to Jesus the mediator of the new covenant:
Alleluia! *Hebrews 12.22-24,28*

10 Great is the Lord and worthy of all praise:
Amen! Praise and glory and wisdom,
thanksgiving and honour, power and might,
be to our God for ever and ever! Amen.
(Alleluia!) *Revelation 5.13*

11 We will praise the name of the Lord;
ascribe greatness to our God.
Lord, open our lips:
and our mouth shall proclaim your praise.
(Alleluia!)

12 The Lord our God, the almighty, reigns.
Let us rejoice and shout for joy,
and give God the glory:
Glory to the Father, and to the Son,
and to the Holy Spirit:
as it was in the beginning, is now,
and shall be for ever. Amen.
(Alleluia!)

13 Jesus also suffered outside the city
to make us holy through his blood.
Let us come to him,
looking for the city which is to come.
Through him we offer our sacrifice of praise to God.
Lord, open our lips:
and our mouth shall proclaim your praise.
Hebrews 3.12,15

14 Let us reflect in silence on our experience of God this week.

We are hard pressed on every side, but not crushed;
perplexed, but not in despair;
persecuted, but not abandoned;
struck down, but not destroyed.
We always carry around in our body the death of Jesus
so that the life of Jesus may be revealed.
We fix our eyes not on what is seen,
but on what is unseen and eternal. *2 Corinthians 4.8-10*

15 The Lord of glory be with you:
The Lord bless you.

(This greeting may be used before or after some of these introductions. 'The Lord of glory' may be replaced by other similar phrases, for example 'The risen Lord', 'The Lord of mercy', 'The Lord of all creation'.)

2 CONFESSIONS

1 **Authorized forms** One of the forms of confession and absolution in the ASB should normally be used. It may sometimes be helpful to vary the form on particular occasions, in which case one of those that follow should be used. They are intended for occasional use only, and should not be printed in a local service book which is used every week.

2 **Invitation to confession** Section 6 in Rite A Holy Communion allows for other suitable words to be used to introduce the confession. Some suggestions are given here. There should be a time for silent reflection between the invitation and the confession.

Advent
When the Lord comes, he will bring to light things now hidden in darkness, and will disclose the purposes of the heart. In that light, we confess our sins.

Christmas
You shall call his name Jesus, for he will save his people from their sins. We know he came into the world to save sinners, so we confess our sins in penitence and faith.

Matthew 1.21

Epiphany
The grace of God has dawned upon the world with healing for all. Though we have grieved him, yet he will heal us if we confess our sins in penitence and faith.

Malachi 4.2

Ash Wednesday
The sacrifice of God is a broken spirit; a broken and contrite heart he will not despise. Our sin is always before us: we acknowledge our transgressions in penitence and faith.

Psalm 51.17

Lent
Christ himself bore our sins in his body on the tree, that we might die to sin and live to righteousness. We know we are healed by his wounds, so we confess our sins.

1 Peter 2.24

Cross
God shows his love for us in this: while we were still sinners Christ died for us. Sure of reconciliation through the death of his Son, we confess our sins to God.

Romans 5.8

Easter
Christ our passover lamb has been offered for us. Let us then rejoice by putting away all malice and evil and confessing our sins with a sincere and true heart.

1 Corinthians 5.7,8

Ascension
Jesus is our high priest, tempted like us, yet without sin. He lives for ever in heaven to intercede for us. Through him we approach the throne of grace with confidence, and confess our sins.

Hebrews 4.15,16

Pentecost
The Spirit of truth will convict the world of guilt about sin, righteousness and judgement. We have grieved the Holy Spirit. We confess our sins in penitence and faith.

John 16.8

Creation
God's whole creation groans. The land produces thorns and thistles and is ready for burning. Our sin affects all around us. We confess that sin in penitence and faith.

Romans 8.22; Genesis 3.18

Word
The word of God is living and active. It judges the thoughts and intentions of the heart. All is open and laid bare before the eyes of him to whom we give account. We confess our sins in penitence and faith.

Hebrews 4.12

City
Jesus saw the city, and wept over it, because it did not recognize the time of God's coming. We confess our part in the self-centredness, blindness and sin of the life of our city.

Luke 19.41

Saints
We run the race set before us, surrounded by a great crowd of witnesses. Therefore let us lay aside every weight, and the sin which clings so closely, bringing them to Jesus in penitence and faith.

Hebrews 12.1

Kingdom
Jesus says, Repent, for the kingdom of heaven is close at hand. So let us turn away from sin and turn to him, confessing our sins in penitence and faith.

Matthew 4.17

Family
Jesus said, Before you offer your gift, go and be reconciled. As brothers and sisters in God's family, we come together to ask our Father for forgiveness.

Matthew 5.24

3 **Kyrie** Sentences may be inserted between the petitions of the Kyrie, to add depth to the penitential section at particular seasons, for example Lent, or on occasions to acts as a substitute for confession. In the latter case, the sentences should be of a penitential character, and be followed by an authorized form of absolution or

May almighty God have mercy on us,
forgive us our sins,
and bring us to everlasting life,
through Jesus Christ our Lord. **Amen.**

The sentences should in any case be short. They may well follow the theme of the readings and opening greeting, and be trinitarian in style. Some examples follow.

Word

May your loving mercy come to me, O Lord,
and your salvation according to your word:

Lord have mercy.
Lord have mercy.

Your word is a lantern to my feet and a light to my path:
Christ have mercy.
Christ have mercy.

O let your mercy come to me that I may live,
for your law is my delight:
Lord have mercy.
Lord have mercy.

City

Lord Jesus, you wept over the sins of your city.
On our city:
Lord have mercy.
Lord have mercy.

Lord Jesus, you heal the wounds of sin and division,
jealousy and bitterness. On us:
Christ have mercy.
Christ have mercy.

Lord Jesus, you bring pardon and peace to the sinner.
Grant us peace:
Lord have mercy.
Lord have mercy.

Spirit

You raise the dead to life in the Spirit:
Lord have mercy.
Lord have mercy.

You bring pardon and peace to the broken in heart:
Christ have mercy.
Christ have mercy.

You make one by your Spirit the torn and divided:
Lord have mercy.
Lord have mercy.

2 2.1 *Incarnation, Christmas*

Lord of grace and truth,
we confess our unworthiness
to stand in your presence as your children.
We have sinned:
forgive – and heal us.

The Virgin Mary accepted your call
to be the mother of Jesus.
Forgive our disobedience to your will.
We have sinned:
forgive – and heal us.

Your Son our Saviour
was born in poverty in a manger.

Forgive our greed and rejection of your ways.
We have sinned:
forgive – and heal us.

The shepherds left their flocks
to go to Bethlehem.
Forgive our self-interest and lack of vision.
We have sinned:
forgive – and heal us.

The wise men followed the star
to find Jesus the King.
Forgive our reluctance to seek you.
We have sinned:
forgive – and heal us.

May the God of all healing and forgiveness
draw you to himself,
that you may behold the glory of his Son,
the Word made flesh,
and be cleansed from all your sins
through Jesus Christ our Lord. **Amen.**

4 2.2 *Lent, Penitence*

Let us admit to God the sin which always confronts us.

Lord God,
we have done evil in your sight;
we have sinned against you alone.
We are sorry and repent.
Have mercy on us according to your love.
Wash away our wrong-doing and cleanse us from our sin.
Renew a right spirit within us
and restore us to the joy of your salvation,
through Jesus Christ our Lord. Amen. *Psalm 51*

May the God of forgiveness
show *you* his mercy,
forgive *you your* sins,
and bring *you* to everlasting life,
through Jesus Christ our Lord. **Amen.**

5 2.3 *Cross, failure in discipleship*

Lord Jesus Christ,
we confess we have failed you as did your disciples,
and we ask for your mercy and your help.

Our selfishness betrays you:
Lord, forgive:
Christ have mercy

We fail to share the pain of your suffering:
Lord, forgive:
Christ have mercy

We run away from those who abuse you:
Lord, forgive:
Christ have mercy

We are afraid of being known to belong to you:
Lord, forgive:
Christ have mercy

May the Father of all mercies
cleanse *you* from *your* sins,
and restore *you* to his service
for the praise and glory of his name,
through Jesus Christ our Lord. **Amen.**

6 2.4 *Resurrection, Heaven, Glory, Transfiguration, Death, Funerals*

O Jesus Christ, risen master and triumphant Lord,
we come to you in sorrow for our sins,
and confess to you our weakness and unbelief:

We have lived by our own strength,
and not by the power of your resurrection.
In your mercy, forgive us:
Lord, hear us and help us.

We have lived by the light of our own eyes,
as faithless and not believing.
In your mercy, forgive us:
Lord, hear us and help us.

God who is both power and love,
forgive *you* and free *you* from *your* sins,
heal and strengthen *you* by his Spirit,
and raise *you* to new life in Christ our Lord.
Amen.

8 2.5 *Trinity*

O Lord our God,
enthroned on high,
filling the whole earth with your glory:
holy, holy, holy is your name.
Our eyes have seen the King,
the Lord almighty;
but our lips are unclean.
We cry to you in our sinfulness
to take our guilt away,
through Jesus Christ our Lord. Amen.

May the Father forgive you
by the blood of the Son
and strengthen you
to live in the power of the Spirit
all your days. **Amen.** *Isaiah 6*

9 2.6 *Creation, Harvest*

We confess our sin, and the sins of our society,
in the misuse of God's creation:

God our Father, we are sorry
for the times when we have used your gifts carelessly,
and acted as though we were not grateful.
Hear our prayer, and in your mercy:
forgive us and help us.

We enjoy the fruits of the harvest,
but sometimes forget that you have given them to us.
Father, in your mercy:
forgive us and help us.

We belong to a people who are full and satisfied,
but ignore the cry of the hungry.
Father, in your mercy:
forgive us and help us.

We are thoughtless,
and do not care enough for the world you have made.
Father, in your mercy:
forgive us and help us.

Some of us store up goods for ourselves alone,
as if there were no God and no heaven.
Father, in your mercy:
forgive us and help us.

The Lord enrich *you* with his grace,
and nourish *you* with his blessing;
the Lord defend *you* in trouble and keep *you* from all evil;
the Lord accept *your* prayers,
and absolve *you* from *your* offences,
for the sake of Jesus Christ, our Saviour. **Amen.**

12 2.7 *City, World and Society*

Lord God, our maker and our redeemer,
this is your world and we are your people:
come among us and save us.

We have wilfully misused your gifts of creation.
Lord, be merciful:
forgive us our sin.

We have seen the ill-treatment of others
and have not gone to their aid.
Lord, be merciful:
forgive us our sin.

We have condoned evil and dishonesty
and failed to strive for justice.
Lord, be merciful:
forgive us our sin.

We have heard the good news of Christ,
but have failed to share it with others.
Lord, be merciful:
forgive us our sin.

We have not loved you with all our heart,
nor our neighbours as ourselves.
Lord, be merciful:
forgive us our sin.

May God who loved the world so much
that he sent his Son to be our Saviour
forgive *you* and make *you* holy to serve him in his world,
through Jesus Christ our Lord. **Amen.**

15 2.8 *Reconciliation*

Let us return to the Lord our God and say to him:

Father,
we have sinned against heaven and against you.
We are not worthy to be called your children.
We turn to you again.
Have mercy on us,
bring us back to yourself
as those who once were dead
but now have life through Christ our Lord. Amen.

Luke 15

May God our Father forgive *you your* sins,
and bring *you* to the fellowship of his table
with his saints for ever. **Amen.**

16 2.9 *Love, Peace*

Come let us return to the Lord and say:

Lord our God,
in our sin we have avoided your call.
Our love for you is like the mist,
disappearing in the heat of the sun.
Have mercy on us.
Bind up our wounds
and bring us back to the foot of the cross,
through Jesus Christ our Lord. Amen.

Hosea 6

May the God of love
bring *you* back to himself,
forgive *you your* sins,
and assure *you* of his eternal love
in Jesus Christ our Lord. **Amen.**

17 2.10 *General*

God our Father,
we come to you in sorrow for our sins:

For turning away from you,
and ignoring your will for our lives:
Father, forgive us:
save us and help us.

For behaving just as we wish,
without thinking of you:
Father, forgive us:
save us and help us.

For failing you by what we do,
and also by what we think and say:
Father, forgive us:
save us and help us.

For letting ourselves be drawn away from you
by temptations in the world about us:
Father, forgive us:
save us and help us.

For living as if we were ashamed
to belong to your Son Jesus:
Father, forgive us:
save us and help us.

May the almighty and merciful Lord
grant *you* pardon and remission of all *your* sins,
time for amendment of life,
and the grace and comfort of his Holy Spirit. **Amen.**

17 2.11 *General*

God, the Father of all mercies,
through his Son Jesus Christ
forgives all who truly repent and believe in him:
by the ministry of reconciliation
which Christ has committed to his Church,
and in the power of the Spirit,
I declare that you are absolved from your sins,
in the name of the Father, and of the Son,
and of the Holy Spirit.

17 2.12 *General*

Mighty and loving God,
in Jesus Christ you have brought us all to new life.
Mend what is broken in us,
and restore us to communion with you

by the power of the Holy Spirit,
that we may follow
our risen Lord and Saviour, Jesus Christ. **Amen.**

17 2.13 *General*

**God our Father,
long-suffering, full of grace and truth.
You create us from nothing and give us life.
You redeem us and make us your children
by baptism.
You do not turn your face from us.
You do not cast us aside.
We confess that we have sinned against you
and our neighbour.
We have wounded your love
and marred your image in us.
For the sake of your Son,
restore us and bring us to your heavenly joy
and peace,
in Jesus Christ our Lord. Amen.**

Almighty God,
who in Jesus Christ has given us
a kingdom that cannot be destroyed,
forgive you your sins,
open your eyes to God's truth,
strengthen you to do God's will
and give you the joy of his kingdom,
through Jesus Christ our Lord. **Amen.**

17 2.14 *General*

**Almighty and most merciful Father,
we have wandered and strayed from your ways
like lost sheep.
We have followed too much the schemes and
desires of our own hearts.
We have offended against your holy laws.
We have left undone those things that we ought
to have done;
And we have done those things that we ought not
to have done;
And there is no health in us.
But you, O Lord, have mercy upon us in our need.**

Spare those who confess their faults.
Restore those who are penitent,
according to your promises declared to mankind
in Christ Jesus our Lord.
And grant, O most merciful Father, for his sake,
that from this time we may live
a disciplined, righteous and godly life,
to the glory of your holy name. Amen.

17 2.15 *General*

Almighty God, Father of our Lord Jesus Christ,
maker of all things, judge of all people,
We acknowledge and confess
the grievous sins and wickedness
which we have so often committed
by thought, word and deed
against your divine majesty,
provoking most justly your anger
and indignation against us.
We do earnestly repent,
and are deeply sorry for these our wrongdoings;
the memory of them weighs us down,
the burden of them is too great for us to bear.
Have mercy upon us,
have mercy upon us, most merciful Father;
For your Son our Lord Jesus Christ's sake,
forgive us all that is past;
And grant that from this time onwards
we may always serve and please you
in newness of life,
to the honour and glory of your name,
through Jesus Christ our Lord. Amen.

17 2.16 *General*

Man born of woman has but a short time to live.[1]
We have our fill of sorrow.
We blossom like a flower and wither away.
We slip away like a shadow and do not stay.

Holy God,
holy and strong,
holy and immortal,
have mercy upon us.

In the midst of life we are in death;
where can we turn for help?
Only to you, Lord,
who are justly angered by our sins.

Holy God,
holy and strong,
holy and immortal,
have mercy upon us.

Shut not your ears to our prayers,
but spare us, O Lord.

Holy God,
holy and strong,
holy and immortal,
have mercy upon us.

You know the secrets of our hearts;
forgive us our sins.

Holy God,
holy and strong,
holy and immortal,
have mercy upon us.

Eternal and merciful judge,
both in life and when we come to die,
let us not fall away from you.

Holy God,
holy and mighty,
holy and merciful Saviour,
do not abandon us to the bitterness of eternal death.

---

[1] *or:* Those born of woman have but a short time to live.

3 WORD

SAMPLES OF NEW LECTIONARY MATERIAL

Around the main festivals, the use of one of the authorised lectionaries will encourage the churches to be telling the same story. Outside that time, in 'ordinary time', it can be acknowledged that churches have differing needs, which may be met by different readings. This sample lectionary is designed to provide mainly for the semi-continuous reading of scripture in short units of five or six weeks, which may be substituted for other authorised readings in 'ordinary time'. It attempts to provide examples of story material suitable both for family services and for adult worship. There is also a sample of thematic material especially suitable for children.

NOTES

1 Though three readings are provided, attention is drawn to the Form of Service (p.17) and Instructions (p.21) for The Service of the Word, which suggest there should *normally* be two readings, but may be only one, if occasion demands. It is better to read two, or one, effectively, and with time given for both preparation and response, than to have three which have to be hurried. The controlling reading, in bold and usually with a title attached, must always be read in some form. If it is not a gospel passage, then the Gospel must also be read if the service is Holy Communion.

2 Where necessary these units may be shortened or amended, to fit the period available, and to avoid having the same or similar readings at the point at which the church moves to one of these units from the ASB or another lectionary, or from one unit to another.

3 The standard form of some of the readings is a short one, often with verses omitted so that an extended story can be included within one reading. The chapter and verse numbers in brackets indicate a longer version which may be the basis for teaching or group study, or be read if there is time, or be the subject of dramatic or visual presentation. Long readings may also be broken up by teaching or songs.

4 Many of the collects in the ASB were chosen to illustrate the theme of the readings and will not be suitable for this lectionary. Other collects should be chosen. The purpose of the collect is to gather the attention of the assembly and to prepare for what is to follow.

5 Some introductory sentences are provided with each unit. Other sentences may also be used.

6 Churches may also wish to design their own reading scheme for a limited period of the year in 'ordinary time', on similar principles. Where they do so they should ensure that an adequate amount of scripture is chosen; that justice is done to the balance of the book and to the general teaching of scripture; that appropriate gospel passages are chosen for the Eucharist; and that the PCC or an appropriate lay group is involved in the decisions.

1 Jacob

In the womb Jacob grasped his brother's heel; as an adult he wrestled with God. *Hosea 12.3*
Blessed is he whose help is the God of Jacob. *Psalm 146.5*

	Old Testament	New Testament	Gospel	Psalm
1	**Gen 25.19-34** (Jacob and Esau 1)	Rom 9.10-16	Luke 1.26-33	105.4-11
2	**Gen 27.11-19 (1-45)** (Jacob and Esau 2)	2 Tim 1.3-7	Mark 3.31-35	50.16-end
3	**Gen 28.10-22 (27.46-28.22)** (Jacob's journey to Bethel)	Rev 7.9-12	John 1.47-51	119.17-24
4	**Gen 29.15-30 (29.1-30)** (Jacob marries)	Eph 5.25-33	Luke 15.11-14	146.3-9
5	**Gen 32.22-33 (32.3-33.16)** (Reconciliation)	2 Cor 5.16-20	Matt 5.3-9	34.3-8

2 Joseph

All things work together for good to those who love God, who are called according to his purpose. *Romans 8.28*
God sent me before you to preserve life. *Genesis 45.5*

	Old Testament	New Testament	Gospel	Psalm
1	**Gen 37.3-13,18-24 (37.1-end)** (An unhappy family)	Rom 8.28-32	John 7.1-6	57.1-7
2	**Gen 39.1-15,20-end (39,40.1-14)** (Joseph in trouble)	Rom 8.33-end	Matt 5.27-30	138
3	**Gen 41.15-25,29-40 (41)** (Joseph, Governor of Egypt)	Rom 12.6-13	Luke 12.27-31	105.16-23

4	**Gen 42.6-25,29-30, 35-36 (42,43)** (Joseph meets his brothers)	Rom 13.1-5	Matt 21.28-32	103.1-12
5	**Gen 44.1-4,14-18, 24-45.9 (44,45)** (Joseph reveals his identity)	Rom 13.8-11	Matt 5.23-26	32
6	**Gen 46.1-7,28-30; 47.7-11 (46.1-7,28-34; 47.1-12)** (A reunited family)	Rom 15.1-6	Matt 6.25-27	126
7	**Gen 50.1-15** (The death of Jacob)	Rom 16.25-27	Luke 10.23-24	128

3 People Jesus met

Everyone who calls out to the Lord for help will be saved. *Romans 10.13*
'Sir, we want to see Jesus.' *John 12.21*

	Old Testament	New Testament	Gospel	Psalm
1	1 Kings 13.3-8	Acts 14.8-11	**Luke 6.6-11** (The man with the paralysed hand)	6
2	2 Kings 5.9-15	Hebrews 11.1-3,6	**Luke 7.1-10** (The Roman Centurion)	103.1-8
3	Hosea 2.19-end	James 2.1-4	**Luke 7.36-50** (Simon the Pharisee)	103.6-18
4	Dan 4.24-27	2 Peter 2.17-end	**Luke 8.26-39** (Legion)	107.10-22
5	Ezek 3.1-3	2 Tim 3.14-end	**Luke 10.38-42** (Martha and Mary)	84
6	Amos 8.11-13	Rev 22.1,2	**John 4.5-26(-34)** (The Samaritan woman)	65
7	Jonah 2.2-9	James 5.13-15	**John 5.1-18** (The man at the pool)	41
8	Isaiah 42.6-9	2 Cor 4.1-6	**John 9.1-12(-end)** (The man born blind)	146

4 Time for a feast

Taste and see how good the Lord is. *Psalm34.8*
Happy are those who have been invited to the wedding-feast of the Lamb. *Revelation 19.9*

	Old Testament	New Testament	Gospel	Psalm
1	Isaiah 55.1-2,10-11	Rom 5.6-11	**Luke 5.27-32 (-35)** (Matthew holds a party)	49
2	Exodus 16.12-18	2 Cor 9.6-10	**Luke 9.10-17** (Feeding of the 5000)	104.24-end
3	Proverbs 25.6,7	1 Peter 5.5-7	**Luke 14.1-14** (Dinner at a Pharisee's house)	113
4	Proverbs 9.1-6	Phil 3.18-end	**Luke 14.15-24** (God's great feast)	23
5	Gen 3.2-6	Acts 16.25-34	**Luke 19.1-10** (Tea and forgiveness)	32.1-7
6	Exodus 12.21-28	1 Cor 10.16,17	**Luke 22.7-20** (The Last Supper)	69.13-22

4 AFFIRMATIONS OF FAITH

One of the authorized affirmations of faith should normally be used: the Apostles' Creed, the Nicene Creed and the Athanasian Creed.

From time to time other affirmations of faith may be used. Only those that follow may be authorized, for occasional use only; they should not be printed in a local service book in the main service for use every week. Compiling statements of the catholic faith is the task of the whole Church, rather than one congregation.

Any suitable words of introduction may be used. These may sometimes indicate the position of the affirmation of faith in the service, as part of the response to the word, or as the climax to praise.

1 We believe in one God,
the Father, the almighty:
maker of heaven and earth,
of all that is, seen and unseen.

We believe in one Lord, Jesus Christ,
the only Son of God,
eternally begotten of the Father:
God from God, Light from Light,
true God from true God,

begotten, not made,
of one Being with the Father:
Through him all things were made.

For us men and for our salvation
he came down from heaven;
by the power of the Holy Spirit
he became incarnate of the Virgin Mary,
and was made man.
For our sake he was crucified under Pontius Pilate;
he suffered death and was buried.

On the third day he rose again
in accordance with the Scriptures:
he ascended into heaven
and is seated at the right hand of the Father.
He will come again in glory
to judge the living and the dead,
and his kingdom will have no end.

We believe in the Holy Spirit.
the Lord, the giver of life,
who proceeds from the Father and the Son.
With the Father and the Son he is worshipped and glorified.
He has spoken through the Prophets.

We believe in one holy, catholic and apostolic Church.
We acknowledge one baptism for the forgiveness of sins:
We look for the resurrection of the dead,
and the life of the world to come. Amen.

2 Do you believe and trust in God the Father,
who made all things?
We believe and trust in him.

Do you believe and trust in his Son Jesus Christ,
who redeemed the world?
We believe and trust in him.

Do you believe and trust in his Holy Spirit,
who gives life to the people of God?
We believe and trust in him.

This is the faith of the Church.
This is our faith.
We believe and trust in one God,
Father, Son and Holy Spirit. Amen.

3 Let us affirm our faith in Jesus Christ the Son of God:

Though he was divine,
he did not cling to equality with God,
but made himself nothing.
Taking the form of a slave,
he was born in human likeness.
He humbled himself,
and was obedient to death –
even the death of the cross.
Therefore God has raised him on high,
and given him the name above every name:
that at the name of Jesus
every knee should bow,

and every voice proclaim
that Jesus Christ is Lord,
to the glory of God the Father. Amen.

Philippians 2.9-11

4 Let us declare our faith
in the resurrection of our Lord Jesus Christ:

Christ died for our sins
in accordance with the scriptures;
he was buried;
he was raised to life on the third day
in accordance with the scriptures;
afterwards he appeared to his followers,
and to all the apostles:
this we have received,
and this we believe. Amen. *1 Corinthians 15.3-7*

5 We say together in faith:

Holy, holy, holy
is the Lord God Almighty,
who was, and is, and is to come.
We believe in God the Father,
who created all things:
for by his will they were created
and have their being.

We believe in God the Son,
who was slain:
for with his blood,
he purchased us for God,
from every tribe and language,
from every people and nation.

We believe in God the Holy Spirit –
the Spirit and the Bride say, 'Come!'
Even so, come Lord Jesus! Amen.

Revelation 4.8,11; 5.9; 22.17

6 Do you believe and trust in God the Father,
who made all things?

I believe in God, the Father almighty,
creator of heaven and earth.

Do you believe and trust in his Son Jesus Christ,
who redeemed the world?

**I believe in Jesus Christ, his only Son, our Lord.
He was conceived by the power of the Holy Spirit
and born of the Virgin Mary.
He suffered under Pontius Pilate,
was crucified, died and was buried.
He descended to the dead.
On the third day he rose again.
He ascended into heaven,
and is seated at the right hand of the Father.
He will come again to judge the living and the dead.**

Do you believe and trust in the Holy Spirit,
who gives life to the people of God?

**I believe in the Holy Spirit,
the holy catholic Church,
the communion of saints,
the forgiveness of sins,
the resurrection of the body,
and the life everlasting.**

This is the faith of the Church.
**This is our faith.
We believe in one God,
Father, Son and Holy Spirit.**

7 We proclaim the Church's faith in Jesus Christ.

**We believe and declare that our Lord Jesus Christ,
the Son of God, is both divine and human;**

God, of the being of the Father,
the only Son from before time began;
human from the being of his mother, born in the world.

**Fully God and fully human;
one human person with mind and body.**

As God he is equal to the Father,
as human he is less than the Father.

**Although he is both divine and human
he is not two beings but one Christ.**

One, not by turning God into flesh,
but by taking humanity into God.

Truly one, not by having a hybrid nature,
but by being one person.

For as mind and body form one human being,
so the one Christ is both divine and human.

The Word became flesh and lived among us;
we have seen his glory,
the glory of the only Son from the Father,
full of grace and truth.

from the Athanasian Creed

8 This reaffirmation of faith may follow a responsive creed,
or may be used independently.

Will you continue in the apostles' teaching and fellowship,
in the breaking of bread, and in the prayers?
With the help of God, I will.

Will you persevere in resisting evil, and,
whenever you fall into sin, repent and return to the Lord?
With the help of God, I will.

Will you proclaim by word and example
the good news of God in Christ?
With the help of God, I will.

Will you seek and serve Christ in all people,
loving your neighbour as yourself?
With the help of God, I will.

Will you acknowledge Christ's authority over human society,
by prayer for the world and its leaders,
by defending the weak, and by seeking peace and justice?
With the help of God, I will.

5 PRAYER

51 **Forms of intercession, responsive prayer and litany**
52 **Post-communion prayers and endings for word services**

NOTES

1 The forms of prayer may replace the intercessions in the Holy Communion, or be used in the prayer section of the Word Service, or after the third collect in Morning or Evening Prayer.

2 These forms are also intended as models for those constructing their own prayers. It may help to note the pattern generally used here, which helps those who do not have the full text in front of them. The prayers may be introduced with a form such as, 'We pray to the Lord, saying . . .' (the words of the response). Or there may be a series of short prayers, or biddings, followed by silence and one of these standard forms:

1 In faith we pray
We pray to you our God

2 Lord, have mercy
Lord, have mercy

3 Lord in your mercy
hear our prayer.

4 Hear us
hear us, good Lord

5 Lord hear us
Lord graciously hear us

6 For. . . let us pray to the Father
in Christ our Lord

7 Jesus, Lord of. . .(a phrase which can be varied)
in your mercy, hear us.

3 Endings for the intercessions

The congregational ending of the Rite A Holy Communion intercessions ('Merciful Father. . .', and the endings of the intercessions that follow, may be replaced by one of these standard endings:

(a) Lord of the Church
hear our prayer,
and make us one in heart and mind
to serve you in Christ our Lord. Amen.

(b) God our Saviour
you know us and love us
and hear our prayer:
keep us in the eternal fellowship
of Jesus Christ our Saviour. Amen.

The last paragraph in Section 21 of the Rite A Holy Communion intercessions ('Rejoicing. . . love') may be replaced by one of the following, which give a weightier ending, and look forward to the communion.

c Bring us all to your heavenly city, to the joyful gathering of thousands of angels, to the assembly of your firstborn, to the spirits of good people made perfect, to Jesus the mediator of the new covenant and to the sprinkled blood that promises peace.
Merciful Father . . .

d Hasten, Lord, the day when people will come from east and west, from north and south, and sit at table in your kingdom and we shall see your Son in his glory.
Merciful Father . . .

e Lord and all-just Judge, grant to us and to all those who long for your appearing the crown of righteousness on the great day of your coming.
Merciful Father . . .

f Fill our hunger with the good food that lasts, the bread of God which comes down from heaven and gives life to the world, with Jesus your Son.
Merciful Father . . .

4 *Alternative introductions to the Lord's Prayer*

1 Let us now pray to the Father, in the words our Saviour gave us.

2 As we look to the coming of God's kingdom, let us say

3 Let us sum up our praise and petitions in the words of Christ, saying

4 Let us once more praise the Father and pray to him in the words of Christ himself.

5 Lord, remember us in your kingdom, as following your teaching we say

6 Following our Lord's teaching, let us say in faith and trust

7 Let us now together say those words which the Lord gave us as the pattern of all prayer.

5 The forms of prayer numbered 52 are provided both as ending prayers for Word Services and post-communion prayers, though sometimes the language will indicate that they can serve only the latter function. The rubric at Section 51 in ASB Rite A provides for other suitable prayers to be used. Some of these prayers (especially those in bold type) are suitable for the whole congregation to join in, when it is possible to print them in full.

Prayer at this point should not be general intercession, but a brief combination of thanksgiving and petition for grace to go out and serve God.

51 *FORMS OF INTERCESSION, RESPONSIVE PRAYER AND LITANY*

1 51.1 *Advent*

In joyful expectation of his coming to our aid
we pray to Jesus, saying,
Maranatha[1]
Come, Lord Jesus.

Come to your Church as Lord and Judge.
We pray for . . .
Help us to live in the light of your coming
and give us a longing for your rule.
Maranatha
Come, Lord Jesus.

Come to your world as King of the nations.
We pray for . . .
Before you rulers will stand in silence.
Maranatha
Come, Lord Jesus.

[1]This word from Revelation 22 means 'Come, Lord Jesus'.

Come to your people with a message of victory and peace.
We pray for . . .
Give us the victory over death, temptation and evil.
Maranatha
Come, Lord Jesus.

Come to us as Saviour and Comforter.
We pray for . . .
Break in to those areas of our lives
where we live with failure and distress,
and set us free to serve you for ever.
Maranatha
Come, Lord Jesus.

Come to us from heaven with power and great glory,
to lift us up to meet you,
with all your saints and angels,
to live with you for ever.
Maranatha
Come, Lord Jesus.

2 51.2 *Incarnation, Christmas, Annunciation, Mary*

Christ, who was born in a stable,
give courage to all who are homeless;
in your mercy
hear our prayer.

Christ, who fled into Egypt,
give comfort to all refugees;
in your mercy
hear our prayer.

Christ, who fasted in the desert,
give relief to all who are starving;
in your mercy
hear our prayer.

Christ, who hung in agony on the cross,
give strength to all who suffer;
in your mercy
hear our prayer.

Christ, who died to save us,
give us your forgiveness;
in your mercy
hear our prayer.

Save us today,
and use us in your loving purpose;
to your glory. Amen.

2 51.3 *Incarnation, Christmas, Annunciation*

To us a child is born, to us a son is given.

Wonderful Counsellor,
give your wisdom to the rulers of the nations.
Lord in your mercy
hear our prayer.

Mighty God,
make the whole world know
that the government is on your shoulders.
Lord in your mercy
hear our prayer.

Everlasting Father,
establish your reign of justice and righteousness
for ever.
Lord in your mercy
hear our prayer.

Prince of peace,
bring in the endless kingdom of your peace.
Lord in your mercy
hear our prayer.

Almighty Lord,
hear our prayer,
and fulfil your purposes in us,
as you accomplished your will
in our Lord Jesus Christ. **Amen.**

2 51.4 *Christmas* [1]

Father, in this holy night your Son our Saviour was born as a human child. Help the Church also to be the Body of Christ.
Lord in your mercy
hear our prayer.

[1] When used during the day the words 'On this holy day' are substituted for 'In this holy night'. Insertions into this intercession should be very brief in order not to imbalance the structure of the prayer.

In this holy night Christians the world over are celebrating his birth. Open our hearts that he may be born in us today.
Lord in your mercy
hear our prayer.

In this holy night there was no room for your Son in the inn.
Protect with your love those who have no home and all who live in poverty.
Lord in your mercy
hear our prayer.

In this holy night Mary in the pain of labour brought your Son to birth. Hold in your hand (. . . and) all who are in any kind of pain or distress today.
Lord in your mercy
hear our prayer.

In this holy night your Christ came as a light shining in the darkness. Bring comfort to (. . . and) all who suffer in the sadness of our world.
Lord in your mercy
hear our prayer.

In this holy night shepherds in the fields heard good tidings of joy. Give us grace to preach the gospel of Christ's redemption.
Lord in your mercy
hear our prayer.

In this holy night the angels sang 'Peace to God's people on earth'. Strengthen those who work for your peace and justice in (. . . and in) all the world.
Lord in your mercy
hear our prayer.

In this holy night strangers saw Mary and Joseph, and the baby lying in the manger. Bless our homes and all whom we love, and help us to live as the holy family.
Lord in your mercy
hear our prayer.

In this holy night heaven is come down to earth and earth is raised to heaven. Keep in safety (. . . and) all

those who have gone through death in the hope of heaven.
Lord in your mercy
hear our prayer.

In this holy night angels and shepherds worshipped at the manger throne. Receive the worship we offer in fellowship with the Blessed Mary and all the saints.
Merciful Father,
accept these prayers
for the sake of your Son,
our Saviour Jesus Christ. Amen.

6 51.5 *Resurrection, Heaven, Glory, Transfiguration, Death*

(In joy and hope let us pray to the Father, saying
in Christ our Lord)

That our risen Saviour may fill us and. . . with the joy of his glorious and life-giving resurrection,
let us pray to the Father
in Christ our Lord.

That isolated and persecuted churches. . . may find fresh strength in the good news of Easter,
let us pray to the Father
in Christ our Lord.

That God may grant us humility to be subject to one another in Christian love . . .
let us pray to the Father
in Christ our Lord.

That he may provide for those who lack food, work, or shelter, and especially . . .
let us pray to the Father
in Christ our Lord.

That by his power war and famine may cease through all the world, and especially . . .
let us pray to the Father
in Christ our Lord.

That he may reveal the light of his presence to the sick, the weak, and the dying, and especially . . . to comfort and strengthen them,
let us pray to the Father
in Christ our Lord.

That he may send the fire of the Holy Spirit upon his people, so that we may bear faithful witness to his resurrection,
let us pray to the Father
in Christ our Lord.

6 51.6 *Resurrection*

(We pray to Jesus who is present with us to eternity, saying
Jesus, Lord of life
in your mercy, hear us.)

Jesus, light of the world,
bring the light and peace of your gospel to the nations
(and especially . . .)
Jesus, Lord of life
in your mercy, hear us.

Jesus, bread of life,
give food to the hungry (and especially. . .)
and nourish us all with your word.
Jesus, Lord of life
in your mercy, hear us.

Jesus, our way, our truth, our life,
be with us and all who follow you in the way,
(and especially. . .)
deepen our appreciation of your truth,
and fill us with your life.
Jesus, Lord of life
in your mercy, hear us.

Jesus, good shepherd who gave your life for the sheep,
surround with your care
those in particular need (and especially. . .)
Jesus, Lord of life
in your mercy, hear us.

Jesus, the resurrection and the life,
we give you thanks
for all who have lived and believed in you
(and especially. . .)
raise us with them to eternal life.
Jesus, Lord of life
in your mercy, hear us,
accept our prayers, and be with us always. Amen.

6 51.7 *Heaven, Death, Funerals and Memorials*

(In our grief we pray,
Lord of mercy
Lord, hear us.)

Almighty God,
you bring your chosen people together in
one communion,
in the body of your Son, Jesus Christ our Lord.
We rejoice in your light and your peace
for your whole Church in heaven and on earth.
Lord of mercy
Lord, hear us.

Give to all who mourn a sure confidence in your
loving care,
that we may cast all our sorrow on you,
and know the consolation of your love.
Lord of mercy
Lord, hear us.

Give your faithful people pardon and peace,
that we may be cleansed from all our sins,
and serve you with a quiet mind.
Lord of mercy
Lord, hear us.

Give us strength to meet the days ahead
in the joyful expectation of eternal life with those
you love.
Lord of mercy
Lord, hear us.

Give to us who are still in our pilgrimage,
and who walk as yet by faith,
your Holy Spirit to lead us
in holiness and righteousness all our days.
Lord of mercy
Lord, hear us.

Give us grace to entrust *N* to your unfailing love
which sustained *him/her* in this life.
Lord of mercy
Lord, hear us.

May all who have been made one with Christ
in his death and in his resurrection
die to sin and rise to newness of life.
Lord of mercy
Lord, hear us.

8 51.8 *Spirit, Pentecost, Gifts, Healing, Baptism and Confirmation*

(We pray to God the Holy Spirit, saying
Holy Spirit, come upon us.)

Come, Holy Spirit, creator, and renew the earth:
Holy Spirit, come upon us.

Come, Holy Spirit, counsellor,
and touch our lips that we may proclaim your word:
Holy Spirit, come upon us.

Come, Holy Spirit, power from on high;
make us agents of peace and ministers of wholeness:
Holy Spirit, come upon us.

Come, Holy Spirit, breath of God,
give life to the dry bones around us,
and make us a living people, holy and free:
Holy Spirit, come upon us.

Come, Holy Spirit, wisdom and truth;
strengthen us to be bold in faith:
Holy Spirit, come upon us.

8 51.9 *Spirit, Pentecost, Gifts, Healing, Baptism and Confirmation*

(We pray that God's Holy Spirit may direct our lives, saying
come to bless us
and fill us with your Spirit.)

'The fruit of the Spirit is
love, joy and peace' –
Father, we know that your world needs love
 and harmony:
come to bless us
and fill us with your Spirit.

'The fruit of the Spirit is
patience, kindness and goodness' –

Father, we know that our world is starved of love
and care:
come to bless us
and fill us with your Spirit.

'The fruit of the Spirit is
faithfulness, gentleness and self-control' –
Father, we know that our world is short of truth
and justice:
come to bless us
and fill us with your Spirit.

Send us out in his power
to live and work to your praise and glory;
through him to whom we belong,
Jesus Christ our Lord. Amen.

8 51.10 *Spirit, Pentecost, Gifts, Healing,*
Baptism and Confirmation

(We pray for God to fill us with his Spirit, saying
Lord, come to bless us
and fill us with your Spirit.)

Generous God, we thank you for the power of your Holy Spirit.
We ask that we may be strengthened to serve you better.
Lord, come to bless us
and fill us with your Spirit.

We thank you for the wisdom of your Holy Spirit.
We ask you to help us understand better your will for us.
Lord, come to bless us
and fill us with your Spirit.

We thank you for the peace of your Holy Spirit.
We ask you to keep us confident of your love and strength wherever you call us to serve you.
Lord, come to bless us
and fill us with your Spirit.

We thank you for the gifts of your Holy Spirit.
We ask you to equip us for the work which you have given us.
Lord, come to bless us
and fill us with your Spirit.

We thank you for the fruit of your Holy Spirit.
We ask you to help us to live lives which are more pleasing to you and show other people the love of Jesus.
Lord, come to bless us
and fill us with your Spirit.

Generous God, you sent your Holy Spirit upon Christ at the river Jordan, and upon the disciples at the feast of Pentecost;
in your mercy fill us with your Spirit,
hear our prayer,
and make us one in heart and mind
to serve you in Christ our Lord. Amen.

10 51.11 *Word*

(We pray to God our Father, saying
Lord, may your word dwell richly in their hearts.)

For all Christian people, knit together by your word of life;
for our bishop, *N*, and for all who teach and guard the faith:
Lord, may your word dwell richly in their hearts.

For those who study and translate the Scriptures:
Lord, may your word dwell richly in their hearts.

For those who are mocked and persecuted for their faith:
Lord, may your word dwell richly in their hearts.

For those who long to know you, and your living Word:
Lord, may your word dwell richly in their hearts.

For those tempted to forsake your way;
for those whose hearts are hardened and unfeeling,
and for those who threaten war:
Lord, may your word dwell richly in their hearts.

For those bowed down with grief, fear or sickness, (especially. . .)
Lord, may your word dwell richly in their hearts.

Giving thanks for those who have died in the faith of Christ, we rejoice (with *N* and) all your saints,

trusting in the promise of your word fulfilled.
Lord of the Church
hear our prayer,
and make us one in heart and mind
to serve you in Christ our Lord. Amen.

11 51.12 *Church, Mission and Ministry, Unity*

(We pray for the use of God's gifts to his Church,
saying
Jesus, Lord of your Church
in your mercy hear us.)

God our Father,
you give us gifts that we may work together
in the service of your Son:

Bless those who lead,
that they may be firm in faith,
yet humble before you:
Jesus, Lord of your Church
in your mercy hear us.

Bless those who teach,
that they may increase our understanding,
and be open to your word for them:
Jesus, Lord of your Church
in your mercy hear us.

Bless those who minister healing,
that they may bring wholeness to others,
yet know your healing in themselves:
Jesus, Lord of your Church
in your mercy hear us.

Bless those through whom you speak,
that they may proclaim your word in power,
yet have their ears open to your gentle whisper:
Jesus, Lord of your Church
in your mercy hear us.

Bless those who work in your world today
that they may live for you, fulfil your purposes,
and seek your kingdom first
in the complexity of their daily lives.
Jesus, Lord of your Church
in your mercy hear us.

Bless those who feel they have no gifts and are not valued,
and those who are powerless by the world's standards,
that they may share their experience
of the work of your Spirit.

Lord of the Church
hear our prayer,
and make us one in heart and mind
to serve you in Christ our Lord. Amen.

13 51.13 *Family*

(We pray for the family of the church, for loving relationships, and for the life of families around us, saying
Jesus, Lord of love
in your mercy, hear us.)

Jesus, born in poverty and soon a refugee,
be with families today who are poor
and live in hunger and want. . .
Jesus, Lord of love
in your mercy, hear us.

Jesus, who grew in wisdom and in favour
with God and the people
in the family of Joseph the carpenter,
bring wisdom and the presence of God
into the work and growth of families today. . .
Jesus, Lord of love
in your mercy, hear us.

Jesus, who blessed marriage in the wedding at Cana,
be with those preparing for marriage
and with those who come to the end of their resources. . .
Jesus, Lord of love
in your mercy, hear us.

Jesus, who healed Peter's mother in law,
bring healing to hurt relationships and families today. . .
Jesus, Lord of love
in your mercy, hear us.

Jesus, who on the cross said,
'Mother, behold your son',
provide today for those who lose their families,
the bereaved and childless, orphans and widows. . .
Jesus, Lord of love
in your mercy, hear us.

Jesus, who on the seashore provided food for
the disciples,
bring the whole Church on earth and in heaven
into your risen presence to eat at the eternal banquet.
Jesus, Lord of love
in your mercy, hear us,
accept our prayers and be with us always. Amen.

13 51.14 *Family*

(We pray for the family of the church and for the life of families around us, saying
Father of all
hear your children's prayer.)

Sovereign Lord, your Son has revealed you as our heavenly Father, from whom every family in heaven and on earth is named.
Father of all
hear your children's prayer.

You have made your church a spiritual family,
a household of faith. Through baptism we are reborn as the brothers and sisters of Christ.
Deepen our unity and fellowship in him.
Father of all
hear your children's prayer.

You sent your Son to give his life as a ransom for the whole human family. Give justice, peace and racial harmony to the world he died to save.
Father of all
hear your children's prayer.

You gave your Son a share in the life of a family in Nazareth. Help us to value our families, to be thankful for them, and to live sensitively within them.
Father of all
hear your children's prayer.

Your Son drew around him a company of friends.
Bring love and joy to all who are alone. Help us all to find in the brothers and sisters of Christ a loving family.
Father of all
hear your children's prayer.

You are the God of the dead as well as of the living. In confidence we remember those of the household of faith who have gone before us. Bring us with them to the joy of your home in heaven.
Father of all
hear your children's prayer.

15 51.15 *Kingdom, Freedom, Reconciliation*

(We pray for the coming of God's kingdom, saying
Father, by your Spirit
bring in your kingdom.)

You came in Jesus to bring good news to the poor,
sight to the blind, freedom to the captives,
and salvation to your people:
anoint us with your Spirit;
rouse us to work in his name:
Father, by your Spirit
bring in your kingdom.

Send us to bring help to the poor
and freedom to the oppressed:
Father, by your Spirit
bring in your kingdom.

Send us to tell the world
the good news of your healing love:
Father, by your Spirit
bring in your kingdom.

Send us to those who mourn,
to bring joy and gladness instead of grief:
Father, by your Spirit
bring in your kingdom.

Send us to proclaim that the time is here
for you to save your people:
Father, by your Spirit
bring in your kingdom.

Lord of the Church
hear our prayer,
and make us one in heart and mind
to serve you in Christ our Lord. Amen.

17 51.16 *A Responsive Intercession*

In faith we pray:
we pray to you our God.

Silence

For all people in their daily life and work:
For our families, friends, and neighbours, and for all those who are alone.

For this community, our country, and the world:
For all who work for justice, freedom, and peace.

For the just and responsible use of your creation:
For the victims of hunger, fear, injustice, and oppression.

For those in danger, sorrow, or any kind of trouble:
For those who minister to the sick, the lonely, and the needy.

For the peace and unity of the Church of God:
For all who proclaim the gospel, and all who seek the truth.

For *N* our bishop, and for all who minister to us:
For all who serve God in his Church.

For our own needs and those of others.

Silence. People may add their own requests.

In faith we pray:
we pray to you our God.

We thank you, Lord, for all the blessings of this life.

Silence. People may add their own thanksgivings.

We give you thanks
and praise your holy name.

We remember those who have died in the faith of Christ. May we, with them, have a place in your eternal kingdom.

Silence. People may add their own requests.

Lord, let your loving kindness be upon them
who put their trust in you.

God our Saviour
you know us and love us
and hear our prayer:
keep us in the eternal fellowship
of Jesus Christ our Saviour. Amen.

17 51.17 *Responsive prayer*

Make your ways known upon earth, Lord God:
your saving power among all peoples.

Renew your church in holiness:
and help us to serve you with joy.

Guide the leaders of this and every nation:
that justice may prevail throughout the world.

Let not the needy be forgotten:
nor the hope of the poor be taken away.

Make us instruments of your peace:
and let your glory be over all the earth.

17 51.18 *Responsive prayer*

In your glory, Lord, protect us by the power of your name:
that we may be one as you are one.

We are in the world but not of it:
protect us from the evil one.

Give us your word and the full measure of your joy:
sanctify us by your truth.

May your Spirit unite us in the love and glory of Father and Son:
may we be one that the world may believe.

As you sent your Son into the world:
so send us, to make your glory known.

John 17.11-18

17 51.19 *Evening Litany*

(We pray to the Lord, saying
in faith we pray:
we pray to you our God.)

That the rest of this day may be holy, peaceful and full of your presence,
in faith we pray:
we pray to you our God.

That the work we have done and the people we have met today may bring us closer to you,
in faith we pray:
we pray to you our God.

(That we may be forgiven our sins and failures,
in faith we pray:
we pray to you our God.)

That we may hear and respond to your call to peace and justice,
in faith we pray:
we pray to you our God.

That you will sustain the faith and hope of those who are lonely, oppressed and anxious,
in faith we pray:
we pray to you our God.

That you will strengthen us in your service, and fill our hearts with longing for your kingdom,
in faith we pray:
we pray to you our God.

God our Saviour
you know us and love us
and hear our prayer:
keep us in the eternal fellowship
of Jesus Christ our Saviour. Amen.

17 51.20 *General*

(We pray for strength to follow Jesus, saying
Saviour, we hear your call:
help us to follow.)

Jesus said: 'If one of you wants to be great,
you must be the servant of the rest.'
Saviour, we hear your call:
help us to follow.

Jesus said: 'Unless you change
and become humble like little children,

you can never enter the kingdom of heaven.'
Saviour, we hear your call:
help us to follow.

Jesus said: 'Happy are the humble;
they will receive what God has promised.'
Saviour, we hear your call:
help us to follow.

Jesus said: 'Be merciful just as your Father is merciful;
love your enemies and do good to them.'
Saviour, we hear your call:
help us to follow.

Jesus said: 'Love one another, just as I love you;
the greatest love a person can have for their friends
is to give their life for them.'
Saviour, we hear your call:
help us to follow.

Jesus said: 'Go to people everywhere
and make them my disciples,
and I will be with you always, to the end of time.'
Saviour, we hear your call:
help us to follow.

God our Saviour
you know us and love us
and hear our prayer:
keep us in the eternal fellowship
of Jesus Christ our Saviour. Amen.

17 51.21 *General*

(We pray for God's grace, saying
Lord, receive our praise
and hear our prayer.)

Lord God, through your grace we are your people:
through your Son you have redeemed us;
in your Spirit you have made us as your own.

We pray for . . . (new Christians, the church . . .)
Make our hearts respond to your love.
Lord, receive our praise
and hear our prayer.

We pray for . . . (the world, society, the local community)
Make our lives bear witness to your glory in the world.
Lord, receive our praise
and hear our prayer.

We pray for . . . (people in need, Christian service)
Make our wills eager to obey,
and our hands ready to heal.
Lord, receive our praise
and hear our prayer.

We give thanks for . . .
Make our voices one with all your people
in heaven and on earth.
Lord of the Church
hear our prayer,
and make us one in heart and mind
to serve you in Christ our Lord. Amen.

52 *POST-COMMUNION PRAYERS AND ENDINGS FOR WORD SERVICES*

1 52.1 *Before Advent*

Almighty God, by your gift
the tree of life was set at the heart of the earthly paradise,
and the bread of life was set at the heart of your Church.
Let this divine nourishment bring us,
not to judgement, but to life eternal,
in Jesus Christ our Lord.

1 52.2 *Advent*

Generous God,
you have fed us at your heavenly table.
Kindle us with the fire of your Spirit
that when Christ comes again
we may shine like lights before his face;
who with you and the Spirit lives for ever.

1 52.3 *Advent*

Loving Father,
your Son Jesus Christ has come to us
in word and Spirit, in bread and cup.
Preserve us from condemnation in body and soul
when he comes to judge the living and the dead,
through Jesus Christ our Lord.

1 52.4 *Advent*

God our guide,
you have fed us with bread from heaven
as you fed your people Israel.
May we who have been spiritually nourished
be ready to follow you all our days;
we ask this in the name of Jesus Christ our Lord.

1 52.5 *Advent*

Gracious Lord,
in this holy sacrament
you give substance to our hope.
Bring us at the last
to that pure life for which we long;
through Jesus Christ our Lord.

1 52.6 *Advent*

Almighty God,
by whose command the order of time
runs its course;
forgive our impatience,
perfect our faith,
and, while we wait for the fulfilment
of your promises,
grant us to have a good hope
because of your word;
through Jesus Christ our Lord.

2 52.7 *Incarnation, Christmas, Annunciation, Mary*

Father of all,
the child born for us is the Saviour of the world.

May he who has made us your children
welcome us into your kingdom,
where he is alive and reigns with you now and for ever.

2 52.8 *Incarnation, Christmas, Annunciation, Mary*

We praise and thank you, Creator God,
for you have not left us alone.
Every year we celebrate your birth, Emmanuel,
every Eucharist we celebrate your death,
in the broken bread and the cup we share,
until that day when we shall see you face to face,
Jesus Christ our Lord.

2 52.9 *Incarnation, Christmas, Annunciation, Mary*

Son of Mary, Son of God,
may we who have joined the worship of the angels
never lose that heavenly vision.
May we who, like the shepherds,
have seen in your birth a new kind of love,
show that love in our lives,
to your praise and glory for ever.

3 52.10 *Epiphany, Light*

God of glory,
you nourish us with your word
which is the bread of life.
Fill us with your Holy Spirit,
that through us the light of your glory
may shine in all the world.
We ask this in the name of Jesus Christ.

4 52.11 *Lent, Penitence*

God of compassion,
through your Son Jesus Christ
you have reconciled your people to yourself.
As we follow his example of prayer and fasting,
may we obey you with willing hearts
and serve one another in holy love;
through Jesus Christ our Lord.

4 52.12 *Lent, Penitence*

Merciful God,
you have called us to your table
and fed us with the bread of life.
Draw us and all people to your Son,
our Saviour Jesus Christ.

4 52.13 *Lent, Penitence*

Eternal God,
comfort of the afflicted and healer of the broken,
you have fed us at the table of life and hope.
Teach us the ways of gentleness and peace,
that all the world may acknowledge
the kingdom of your Son Jesus Christ our Lord.

4 52.14 *Lent, Penitence*

Faithful God,
may we who share this banquet
glory in the cross of our Lord Jesus Christ,
our salvation, life and hope,
who reigns as Lord now and for ever.

4 52.15 *Lent, Penitence*

God of our pilgrimage,
you have led us to the living water.
Refresh and sustain us
as we go forward on our journey,
in the name of Jesus Christ our Lord.

5 52.16 *Cross*

Jesus, Son of God, our true and only Saviour:
you died like a criminal on a cross;
but you are God who forgives.
Once broken, helpless and in pain,
you are God in whom there is hope.
You have shown us a love beyond words:
give us your forgiveness, hope and love.

6 52.17 *Resurrection, Heaven, Glory, Transfiguration, Death, Funerals*

God of our salvation,
you have restored us to life,
you have brought us back again into your love,
by the triumphant death
and resurrection of Christ.
Continue to heal us,
as we go to live and work
in the power of your Spirit,
to your praise and glory.

6 52.18 *Resurrection, Heaven, Glory, Transfiguration*

God of truth,
we have seen with our eyes
and touched with our hands
the bread of life.
Strengthen our faith
that we may grow in love for you
and for each other;
through Jesus Christ our risen Lord.

6 52.19 *Heaven*

**God and Father of our Lord Jesus Christ,
bring us to the dwelling which your Son
is preparing for all who love you.
Give us the will each day
to live in life eternal.**

**Let our citizenship be in heaven
with your blessed and beloved,
the whole company of the redeemed;
and with countless angels,
praising, worshipping and adoring him
who sits upon the throne for ever and ever.
Amen.**

To him who is able to keep us from falling and to present us without blemish before the presence of his glory with rejoicing, to the only God, our Saviour, through Jesus Christ our Lord, be glory, majesty, dominion and authority, before all time and now and for ever.

8 52.20 *Spirit, Pentecost, Gifts, Healing, Baptism and Confirmation*

Holy and blessed God,
as you give us the body and blood of your Son,
fill us with your Holy Spirit,
that we may honour you not only with our lips
but also in our lives.
This we ask in the name of Jesus Christ our Lord.

8 52.21 *Spirit, Pentecost, Gifts, Healing, Baptism and Confirmation*

Father, in baptism we die to sin,
rise again to new life,
and find our true place in your living body.
Send us out sealed in Christ's blood of the new covenant,
to bring healing and reconciliation to this wounded world,
through Jesus Christ our Lord.

8 52.22 *Spirit, Pentecost, Gifts, Healing, Baptism and Confirmation*

God of power,
may the boldness of your Spirit transform us,
may the gentleness of your Spirit lead us,
may the gifts of your Spirit
equip us to serve and worship you
now and always.

9 52.23 *Creation, Harvest, Bread, Vine*

Creator God
you give seed for us to sow,
and bread for us to eat;
make us thankful for what we have received;
make us able to do those generous things
which supply your people's needs;
so all the world may give you thanks and glory.

10 52.24 *Word*

God from whom all wisdom comes,
thank you for feeding us by your word and Spirit;
help us to understand ourselves, our world and you;
and give those who teach us
commitment to truth and respect for doubt,
through Jesus Christ our Lord.

10 52.25 *Word*

Lord God,
you feed us with the living bread from heaven;
you renew our faith,
increase our hope,
and strengthen our love.
Teach us to hunger
for Christ who is the true and living bread,
and to live by every word
that comes from your mouth,
through Jesus Christ our Lord.

11 52.26 *Church, Mission and Ministry, Unity*

Eternal Giver of love and life,
your Son Jesus Christ has sent us into all the world
to preach the gospel of his kingdom.
Confirm us in this mission,
and help us to live the good news we proclaim,
through Jesus Christ our Lord.

11 52.27 *Church, Mission and Ministry, Unity*

Lord God,
the source of truth and love,
keep us faithful to the apostles' teaching and fellowship,
united in prayer and the breaking of bread,
and one in joy and simplicity of heart,
in Jesus Christ our Lord.

11 52.28 *Church, Mission and Ministry, Unity*

Keep us, Father, in this community of faith,
the Church of your Son Jesus Christ,

and help us to confess him as Messiah and Lord
in all we say and do.
We ask this in his name.

11 52.29 *Church, Mission and Ministry, Unity*

Lord God,
thank you for the unity you give us in your presence:
draw your Church together
into one great company of disciples,
together following our Lord Jesus Christ
into every walk of life,
together serving him in his mission to the world,
and together witnessing to his love
on every continent and island,
in the power of your Spirit,
to your praise and glory.

11 52.30 *Unity*

Great God, you are one God,
and you bring together what is scattered
and mend what is broken.
Unite us with the scattered peoples of the earth
that we may be one family of your children.
Bind up all our wounds,
and heal us in spirit
that we may be renewed as disciples
of Jesus Christ, our Master and Saviour.

11 52.31 *Unity*

Fill us, good Lord, with your Spirit of love;
and as you have fed us with the one bread of heaven,
so make us one in heart and mind,
in Jesus Christ our Lord. Amen.

11 52.32 *Mission, Unity*

Eternal God and Father,
whose Son at supper
prayed that his disciples might be one,

as he is one with you;
draw us closer to him,
that in common love and obedience to you
we may be united to one another
in the fellowship of the Spirit,
that the world may believe that he is Lord,
to your eternal glory;
through Christ our Lord.

12 52.33 *City, World and Society*

Father of Lights,
from whom comes every good and perfect gift:
keep us in the light of Christ,
to shine in your world,
that all may believe in you
through Jesus Christ our Lord.

13 52.34 *Family*

Father of all, you gathered us here
around the table of your Son;
we have shared this meal with saints
and the whole fellowship of the household of God.
In that new world
where the fullness of your peace will be revealed,
gather people of every race, language and way of life
to share in the one eternal banquet
of Jesus Christ the Lord.

14 52.35 *Saints*

Lord of heaven,
in this Eucharist you have brought us near
to an innumerable company of angels,
and to the spirits of saints made perfect.
As in this food of our earthly pilgrimage
we have shared their fellowship,
so may we come to share their joy in heaven,
for ever and ever.

16 52.36 *Love, Peace*

Lord God,
you hold both heaven and earth in peace.

Let the design of your great love
shine on the waste of our rages and sorrows,
and give peace to your Church,
peace among nations,
peace in our homes, and peace in our hearts,
in Jesus Christ our Lord.

17 52.37 *General*

Heavenly Father,
we share together
the blessing of your presence.
Give us in this life knowledge of your truth,
and in the world to come life everlasting;
through Jesus Christ your Lord.

17 52.38 *General*

We have broken your bread, Lord.
We have received your life.
By the power of your Spirit
keep us always in your love.

17 52.39 *General*

Eternal Father,
we thank you for refreshing us
with these heavenly gifts:
may our communion
strengthen us in faith
build us up in hope
and make us grow in love,
for the sake of Jesus Christ our Lord.

17 52.40 *Morning*

Eternal God,
our beginning and our end,
be our starting point and our haven,
and accompany us in this day's journey.
Use our hands
to do the work of your creation

and use our lives
to bring others the new life you give this world
in Jesus Christ, Redeemer of all.

17 52.41 *Evening*

Gracious God,
you have given us much today;
grant us also a thankful spirit.
Into your hands we commend ourselves
and those we love.
Stay with us, and when we take our rest
renew us for the service of your Son Jesus Christ.

17 52.42 *Evening*

In darkness and in light,
in trouble and in joy,
help us, heavenly Father,
to trust your love,
to serve your purpose,
and to praise your name,
through Jesus Christ our Lord.

17 52.43 *Evening*

Lord, you have brought us through this day
to a time of reflection and rest.
Calm us,
and give us your peace to refresh us.
Keep us close to Christ
that we may be closer to one another
because of his perfect love.
In his name we pray.

17 52.44 *Evening*

God, you are everything to us,
giving us life,
filling it with love,
and setting us free from sin
that we might live in love.
Take the work of our hands this day,
and let good come of it;
take our lives,

give us your peace,
and renew us in the service of Jesus Christ
our Lord.

17 52.45 *General*

We thank you, Lord,
that you have fed us in this sacrament,
united us with Christ,
and given us a foretaste
of the heavenly banquet.

17 52.46 *General*

May holy Wisdom,
kind to humanity,
steadfast, sure and free,
the breath of the power of God –
may she who makes all things new, in every age,
enter our souls, and make us friends of God,
through Jesus Christ.

6 PRAISE

61 Short acclamations and responses
62 Acclamations and responses
63 Longer acclamations and responsive scriptures
64 Proper prefaces
65 Thanksgivings
66 Songs

61 *SHORT ACCLAMATIONS AND RESPONSES*

These may be used at the beginning or end of worship. They may be used after a reading, or repeated at various points in a service as a reminder of the theme.

1 61.1 Christ in you, the hope of glory:
This is the gospel we proclaim! *Colossians 1.27*

2 61.2 The Word was made flesh and lived among us:
and we have seen his glory. *John 1.14*

2 61.3 The Son of man came not to be served but to serve:
to give up his life as a ransom for many. *Mark 10.45*

3 61.4 Christ has brought us out of darkness:
to dwell in the light of his glory. *1 Peter 2.9*

4 61.5 Jesus is the Lamb of God:
who takes away the sins of the world.
Alleluia! *John 1.29*

5 61.6 God forbid that we should glory:
save in the cross of Christ our Lord. *Galatians 6.14*

6 61.7 Jesus is the resurrection and the life:
Those who believe in him shall never die.
Alleluia! *John 11.25*

7 61.8 We have a great high priest who has passed through the heavens:
we come boldly to the throne of grace.
Hebrews 4.14,16

8 61.9 Jesus said, 'Receive the Spirit:
as the Father sent me, so I send you.' *John 20.21,22*

8 61.10 We have died together with Christ:
We rise united with him. *Romans 6.5*

10 61.11 Your word is a lantern to my feet:
and a light upon our path. *Psalm 119.105*

11 61.12 There is one body and one Spirit:
one Lord, one faith, one baptism. *Ephesians 4.4,5*

11 61.13 The love of Christ compels us:
We are ambassadors for him. *2 Corinthians 5.14,20*

17 61.14 Rejoice in the Lord always!
and again I say 'Rejoice'. *Philippians 4.4*

62 *ACCLAMATIONS AND RESPONSES*

NOTES

1 Most of these may be used in place of the versicles and responses in a Word Service, or at the beginning of worship.

2 Sections marked ★ may be said together as a canticle, rather than in responsive form.

1 62.1★ *Advent*

Restore us, Lord God of hosts:
show us the light of your face, turned towards us.

Will you not give us life again:
that your people may rejoice in you?

Show us your mercy, O Lord:
and grant us your salvation.

Blessed is the King who comes in the name of the Lord!
Peace in heaven and glory in the highest.

2 62.2★ *Incarnation*

Blessed be the Lord, the God of Israel:
may all the earth be filled with his glory.

Light has sprung up for the righteous:
and joyful gladness for those who are faithful.

Glory to God in the highest:
and peace to his people on earth.

3 62.3 *Epiphany*

Blessed are you, Lord our God, King of the universe!
from the rising of the sun to its setting
your name is proclaimed in all the world.

When the time had fully come
your unconquered Sun of Righteousness
in whom the fullness of your glory dwells
called us out of darkness into his own marvellous light.

You gave him as a light to the nations,
and by the outpouring of his anointing Spirit
you establish us as your royal priesthood.

According to the riches of his glory
may we be strengthened though his Spirit
that, rooted and grounded in love,
our lives may be a witness to your truth,
and our lips never cease to proclaim your praise,
now and for ever. Amen.

4 62.4* *Lent, Penitence*

Cast your burden upon the Lord:
and he will sustain you.

Create in us clean hearts, O God:
and renew a right spirit within us.

Cast us not away from your presence:
and take not your Holy Spirit from us.

Give us the joy of your saving help again:
and sustain us with your life-giving Spirit.

Blessed be the Lord day by day:
the God of our salvation, who bears our burdens.

5 62.5* *Cross*

Christ became obedient unto death for us:
even death upon a cross.

He was pierced for our sins:
bruised for no fault but ours.

His punishment has brought us peace:
and by his wounds we are healed.

Worthy is the Lamb that was slain
to receive power and riches and wisdom:
strength, honour, glory, and praise. Amen.

5 62.6 *Cross*

O Lord, open my lips,
and my mouth shall proclaim your praise.

When we were still helpless
Christ died for the ungodly.

The proof of God's amazing love is this:
while we were still sinners, Christ died for us.

Romans 5.6,8

5 62.7 *Baptism, Cross*

Since we have died with Christ,
we believe that we will also live with him.

For we know that Christ has been raised from death
and will never die again.

We were baptized into union with his death;
and have set out on a new life with the risen Christ.

6 62.8 *Resurrection*

Alleluia! Christ is risen:
He is risen indeed. Alleluia!

Praise the God and Father of our Lord Jesus Christ:
He has given us new life and hope!
He has raised Jesus from the dead!

God has claimed us as his own:
He has brought us out of darkness!
He has made us light to the world!

Alleluia! Christ is risen:
He is risen indeed. Alleluia!

6 62.9 *Resurrection*

Christ is risen:
He is risen indeed. Alleluia!

Blessed are those who have not seen him and yet have believed:
He is our Lord and our God. Alleluia!

We have seen his glory:
glory as of the only Son from the Father, full of grace and truth. Alleluia!

The Lord says to us 'Do you love me?'
Our hearts reply 'You know that we love you'. Alleluia!

Jesus says 'Anyone who comes to me shall never hunger'.
and 'whoever believes in me shall never thirst'. Alleluia!

This is the Lamb of God:
who takes away the sins of the world. Alleluia!

Jesus is the resurrection and the life:
Those who believe in him shall never die. Alleluia!

Yes - Christ is risen:
He is risen indeed. Alleluia!

7 62.10 *Resurrection*

Here are words you may trust
Remember Jesus Christ, risen from the dead:
He is our salvation, our eternal glory.

If we die with him, we shall live with him:
if we endure we shall reign with him.

If we deny him, he will deny us:
if we are faithless, he keeps faith.

For he has broken the power of death:
and brought life and immortality to light through the gospel.

2 Timothy 2.11-13

7 62.11★ *Trinity*

You are worthy, our Lord and God:
to receive glory and honour and power.

For you created all things:
and through your will they have their being.

You are worthy, Lamb of God, for you were slain:
and by your blood you ransomed us for God.

From every tribe and tongue and people and nation:
you made us a kingdom of priests to serve our God.

To him who sits upon the throne, and to the Lamb:
be blessing and honour and glory and might for ever and ever. Amen.

Revelation 4.11; 5.9,10,13

8 62.12★ *Spirit, Pentecost, Gifts, Healing, Baptism and Confirmation*

There are varieties of gifts:
but the same Spirit.

There are varieties of service:
but the same Lord.

There are different kinds of working:
but the same God is at work in all.

1 Corinthians 12.4-6

8 62.13★ *Spirit, Pentecost, Gifts, Healing, Baptism and Confirmation*
(may be used with 62.12 above)

There is one body, one Spirit, one hope in God's call:
One Lord, one faith, one baptism.

There is one God, Father of all, over all and in all:
to whom Christ ascended on high.

And through his Spirit he gives us gifts:
Some are apostles, some are his prophets;

Evangelists, pastors and teachers he gives us:
So we can minister together

To build up his body:
to be mature in the fullness of Christ.

Ephesians 4.4-13

8 62.14★ *Spirit, Pentecost, Gifts, Healing, Baptism and Confirmation*

The love of God has been poured into our hearts,
through the Holy Spirit who has been given to us:
we dwell in him and he in us.

Give thanks to the Lord and call upon his name:
make known his deeds among the peoples.

Sing to him, sing praises to him:
and speak of all his marvellous works.

Holy, holy, holy, is the Lord God almighty:
who was and is and is to come!

8 62.15★ *Spirit, Pentecost, Gifts, Healing, Baptism and Confirmation*

I saw water flowing from the threshold of the temple:
where the river flows everything will spring to life.

On the banks of the river grow trees bearing every kind of fruit:
their leaves will nor wither nor their fruit fail.

Their fruit will serve for food,
their leaves for the healing of the nations:
for the river of the water of life
flows from the throne of God and of the Lamb.

from Ezekiel 47 and Revelation 22

8 62.16 *Spirit*

Now that we have been put right with God through faith,
we have peace with God through our Lord Jesus Christ.

He has brought us by faith into the grace of God.
We rejoice in the hope of sharing God's glory!

This hope does not deceive us
for God has poured his love into our hearts by the gift of his Spirit.

Romans 5.1-2

9 62.17 *Creation*

Lord, we are clay,
and you are the potter.

We are all the work of your hand.
Do not remember our sins for ever.

Look upon us in your mercy
for we are your people.

12 62.18* *City, World and Society*

A city on a hill canot be hidden:
We are the light of the world.

Jesus said, I am the light of the world:
We follow him with the light of life.

Light has come into the world:
We loved darkness rather than light.

The light exposes the deeds of the evil:
But we have come into the light and live by the truth,

So all can see what we do:
through God in the light of his glory. Alleluia !

Matthew 5.14; John 3.19-21; 8.12

14 62.19* *Saints*

Great is the Lord and greatly to be praised:
There is no end of his greatness.

One generation shall praise your works to another:
And shall declare your power.

All your works praise you, Lord:
And your faithful servants bless you.

They make known the glory of your kingdom:
And speak of your power.

My mouth shall speak the praise of the Lord:
Let all flesh bless his holy name for ever and ever.
from Psalm 145

14 62.20★ *Saints*

Blessed are you, Lord our God, King of the universe!
You have given us a share
in the inheritance of the saints in light.

In the darkness of this age
your saints proclaim the glory of your kingdom.
Chosen as lights in the world,
they surround our steps as we journey on
towards that eternal city of light
where they sing the triumphal song.

Open our eyes to behold your glory
and free our tongues to join our song with theirs.
Great and wonderful are your deeds,
Lord God Almighty;

Just and true are your ways, King of the ages.
To you be praise and glory, now and for ever.
Amen.

14 62.21 *Saints*

In the city of God, night shall be no more;
the people of God need no light of lamp or sun,

for the Lord God will be their light,
and they will reign for ever and ever.
Revelation 22.5

16 62.22★ *Love*

This is love, not that we loved God:
but that he loved us and sent his Son.

He is the sacrifice for our sins:
that we might live through him.

If God loves us so much:
we ought to love one another.

If we love one another:
God lives in us. *1 John 4.12*

17 62.23 *Light, Evening*

Jesus Christ is the light of the world,
light no darkness can quench.

Stay with us, Lord, for it is evening,
and the day is almost over.

Even the darkness is not dark for you,
and the night shines like the day;

Let your light scatter the darkness
and fill your church with your glory.

John 1.5; 8.12; Luke 24.29

17 62.24 *Light, Evening*

God is light.
In him there is no darkness.

If we live in the light,
as God is in the light,

we have fellowship with one another,
and the blood of Jesus, his Son, purifies us from all sin.

1 John 1.5,7

17 62.25 *Evening, Creation*

Blessed are you, Lord God, King of the universe!
Your word brings on the dusk at evening

Your wisdom creates both night and day.
You determine the cycles of time,

arrange the succession of seasons,
and establish the stars in their heavenly courses.
Lord of the starry hosts is your name.

Living and eternal God, rule over us always.
Blessed be the Lord, whose word makes evening fall.

17 62.26 *General*

Let us give thanks to the God of our Lord Jesus Christ,
who has blessed us in Christ with every spiritual blessing.

Before the world was made, God chose us in Christ,
that we might be holy and blameless before him.

Let us praise God for the glory of his grace,
for the free gift he gave us in his dear Son.

Ephesians 1.3-6

17 62.27 *Praise*

O Lord, open my lips;
And my mouth shall proclaim your praise.

Sing psalms, hymns and sacred songs;
let us sing to God with thanksgiving in our hearts.

Let everything you do or say be done in the name of the Lord Jesus,
giving thanks to God through Jesus Christ.

Colossians 3.16-17

63 LONGER ACCLAMATIONS AND RESPONSIVE SCRIPTURES

NOTES

1 **Songs** Sections marked * may be said together as a song, rather than in responsive form.

2 **Responsive scriptures**, marked †, may be used in the Ministry of the Word, where they may take the place of a song or reading; or they may, with appropriate texts, be used as thanksgivings, for instance as the climax to a Word Service. Others may be added to the selection here, provided care is taken to choose texts, and versions, which are rhythmical, and to choose responses which are short, easy to say congregationally, and contribute to reflection on the inner meaning of the scripture.

3 **Praise responses** The following four responses should be regarded as standard responses, to be used after biddings or in litanies in a similar way to the Prayer responses (**5**, note 2):

1 Praise him:
Praise him!

2 We give you thanks:
We praise your holy name.

3 Father in heaven:
We give you thanks and praise.

4 Jesus, Lord of all:
We worship and adore you.

(the first line of this may be appropriately varied, within the same rhythm, e.g. Jesus, Son of God; Jesus, born of Mary; Jesus, conqueror of death; Jesus, servant of all; Jesus, Lord of heaven; Jesus, redeemer of the world. . .)

1 63.1† *Advent*

My soul is waiting for the Lord;
in his word is my hope.

My soul is waiting for the Lord;
in his word is my hope.

Out of the depths have I called to you, O Lord.
Lord, hear my voice.
In his word is my hope.

There is forgiveness with you;
therefore you shall be feared.
In his word is my hope.

My soul is longing for the Lord,
more than those who watch for daybreak.
In his word is my hope.

O Israel, wait for the Lord,
for with the Lord there is mercy:
In his word is my hope.

Glory to the Father, and to the Son,
and to the Holy Spirit:
My soul waits for the Lord;
in his word is my hope. *Psalm 130*

3 63.2* *Epiphany, Light*

Jesus Christ is the light of the world:
light no darkness can quench.
Stay with us, Lord, for it is evening:
and the day is almost over.
Let your light scatter the darkness:
and fill your church with your glory.

You, Christ, are the King of glory:
You are the everlasting Son of the Father.
When you drew the sting of death:
You opened heaven to all who trust in you.
Come then, we pray, to the aid of your people:
We are bought at the price of your own precious blood.
When you make up the number of your saints:
Bring us with them to glory for ever. Amen.

4 63.3 *Lent, Penitence*

Incline your ear to me;
make haste to answer when I call.

Incline your ear to me;
make haste to answer when I call.

Lord, hear my prayer,
and let my cry come before you:
Make haste to answer when I call.

Hide not your face from me
in the day of my trouble:
Make haste to answer when I call.

You, Lord, endure for ever,
and your name from age to age:
Make haste to answer when I call.

You will arise and have compassion on Zion,
for it is time to have pity on her:
Make haste to answer when I call.

Glory to the Father, and to the Son,
and to the Holy Spirit:
Incline your ear to me;
make haste to answer when I call.

Psalm 102.1,2,12,13

5 63.4 *Cross*

Father, you loved the world so much that you sent
your only Son to die that we might live through him.
‡(For his words from the cross, we bring you thanks and praise:)

('Forgive . . .')
He forgave in the face of bitter hatred.
We give you thanks.
We praise your holy name.

('Today you shall be with me in paradise.')
He promised heaven to the forgiven sinner.
We give you thanks.
We praise your holy name.

('Mother . . . behold your Son')
He loved his mother to the last.
We give you thanks.
We praise your holy name.

('I thirst . . .')
He shared in our physical suffering and longing.
We give you thanks.
We praise your holy name.

('Why have you forsaken me?')
He entered into our desolation and suffering.
We give you thanks.
We praise your holy name.

('It is finished!')
He completed his saving work,
and made the new covenant of love between God
and his world.
We give you thanks.
We praise your holy name.

('Into your hands I commit my spirit.')
He won the victory over sin and death for ever.
We give you thanks.
We praise your holy name.

---

‡The quotations in brackets are best used only when there has been specific reference in the service to Jesus' words from the cross. Not every section need be used.

6 63.5 *Resurrection*

Our Lord Jesus Christ, risen from death,
we praise you for changed lives and new hopes at Easter.

You come to Mary in the garden, and turn her tears into joy.
For your love and mercy we give you thanks.
We praise your holy name.

You come to the disciples in the upper room,
and turn their fear into courage.
For your love and mercy we give you thanks.
We praise your holy name.

You come to the disciples by the lakeside,
and turn their failure into faith.
For your love and mercy we give you thanks.
We praise your holy name.

You come to the disciples on the Emmaus road,
and turn their despair into hope.
For your love and mercy we give you thanks.
We praise your holy name.

You come to your people now,
and turn our weakness into triumph.
For your love and mercy we give you thanks.
We praise your holy name.

6 63.6 *Resurrection*

Let the voice of God's praise resound;
he is the source of our life.

Let the voice of God's praise resound;
he is the source of our life.

Be joyful in God, all you lands;
sing the glory of his name:
He is the source of our life.

Come now and see the work of God,
how wonderful he is toward all people:
He is the source of our life.

He turned the sea into dry land,
so that they went through the water on foot:
He is the source of our life.

There we rejoiced in him.
In his might he rules for ever:
He is the source of our life.

Glory to the Father, and to the Son,
  and to the Holy Spirit:
Let the voice of God's praise resound;
he is the source of our life. *Psalm 66.4-8*

6 63.7 *Resurrection, Heaven, Glory, Transfiguration, Death, Funerals*

Lord, we remember you, our creator.
You sent your Son to win the victory
over death for ever.

Before sun and light and moon and stars grow dark,
and the clouds return after the rain:

Lord, we remember you, our creator.
You sent your Son to win the victory
over death for ever.

We see the day when those who keep the house tremble
and strong women are bowed;
when men grind no longer at the mill,
because day is darkening at the windows
and the street doors are shut:

Lord, we remember you, our creator.
You sent your Son to win the victory
over death for ever.

When the sound of the mill is faint,
when the voice of the bird is silenced,
and song notes are stilled,
when to go uphill is an ordeal
and a walk is something to dread:

Lord, we remember you, our creator.
You sent your Son to win the victory
over death for ever.

Yet the trees are in flower
and insects are fat with food,
while we go to our everlasting home,
and the mourners are already walking up and down
  in the street:

Lord, we remember you, our creator.
You sent your Son to win the victory over death for ever.

Before the silver cord has snapped,
or the golden lamp has broken,
or the pitcher shattered at the spring,
or the pulley cracked at the well,

Lord, we remember you, our creator.
You sent your Son to win the victory over death for ever.

Before the dust returns to the earth
and the breath to God who gave it:

Lord, we remember you, our creator.
You sent your Son to win the victory over death for ever: Alleluia !

Ecclesiastes 12.1-8

9 63.8 *Creation*

You are the eternal Father:
all creation worships you.

Who decided the dimensions of the earth?
Or who stretched the measuring line across it?
What supports its pillars at their bases?
Who laid its cornerstone
when all the stars of the morning were singing with joy,
and the children of God in chorus were chanting praise?

You are the eternal Father:
all creation worships you.

Who pent up the sea behind closed doors
when it leapt tumultuous out of the womb,
when I wrapped it in a robe of mist
and made black clouds its swaddling bands;
when I marked the bounds it was not to cross
and made it fast with a bolted gate?
Come thus far, I said, and no farther:
here your proud waves shall break.

You are the eternal Father:
all creation worships you.

Have you ever visited the place where the snow is kept,
or seen where the hail is stored up,

which I keep for times of stress,
for days of battle and war?

You are the eternal Father:
all creation worships you.

From which direction does the lightning fork
when it scatters sparks over the earth?
Who carves a channel for the downpour,
and hacks a way for the rolling thunder,
so that rain may fall on lands where no-one lives,
and the deserts void of human dwelling,
giving drink to the lonely wastes
and making grass spring where everything was dry?

You are the eternal Father:
all creation worships you.

Have the rain or dew a father?
Who is mother of the ice or frost
which turn the water to stone?

You are the eternal Father:
all creation worships you. *Job 38*

11 63.9 *Church, Mission and Ministry, Unity*

Sovereign Lord, creator of heaven and earth and sea,
and everything in them:
We are your people, we give you thanks.
We praise your holy name.

You shake us and fill us with your Spirit,
You stretch out your hand to heal,
to do signs and wonders through the name of Jesus.
We are your people, we give you thanks.
We praise your holy name.

He is the author of life,
handed over to be killed for us.
You raised him from the dead,
and made us whole in him.
We are your people, we give you thanks.
We praise your holy name.

Not many of us are wise by human standards,
not many are influential,
not many of noble birth.

We are your people, we give you thanks.
We praise your holy name.

You choose the foolish to shame the wise,
you choose the weak to shame the strong,
the lowly and despised,
so no one may boast before you.
We are your people, we give you thanks.
We praise your holy name.

Your strength is made perfect in our weakness.
Your grace is enough for us.
We are your people, we give you thanks.
We praise your holy name.

Acts 4.24,30,31; 3.15,13;
1 Corinthians 1.26-29; 2 Corinthians 12.9

17 63.10 *General*

In my mouth he has put a new song:
Praise to our God!

In my mouth he has put a new song:
Praise to our God!

I waited patiently upon the Lord;
he stooped to me and heard my cry:
Praise to our God!

Many shall see, and stand in awe,
and put their trust in the Lord:
Praise to our God!

I love to do your will, Lord God;
your law is deep in my heart:
Praise to our God!

I proclaimed righteousness in the great congregation;
behold, I did not restrain my lips:
Praise to our God!

Glory to the Father, and to the Son,
and to the Holy Spirit.
In my mouth he has put a new song:
Praise to our God! *Psalm 40*

17 63.11 *Morning*

The Lord is with us, he is our stronghold;
God will help at the break of day.

The Lord is with us, he is our stronghold;
God will help at the break of day.

God is our refuge and strength,
a very present help in trouble:
God will help at the break of day.

We will not fear, though the earth be moved,
and though the mountains be toppled into the depths of the sea:
God will help at the break of day.

Come now and look upon the works of the Lord,
what awesome things he has done on earth:
God will help at the break of day.

Be still and know that I am God;
I will be exalted among the nations;
I will be exalted in the earth:
God will help at the break of day.

Glory to the Father, and to the Son,
and to the Holy Spirit.
The Lord is with us, he is our stronghold:
God will help at the break of day. *Psalm 46*

17 63.12 *Dedication*

We offer to God our skills and our service,
our lives and our worship.

O God, you are the source of life and health and strength,
and in Jesus Christ you have given us a Saviour and a friend.

For the love that made you enter our world in Jesus
to share our joys and sorrows
and to die for our sin — Father
receive the gift of our love.

For the forgiveness you promise
to all who confess their sins
and trust in his sacrifice on the cross — Father
receive the gift of our penitence.

For the hope of eternal life we have in Christ
because you raised him from the dead — Father
receive the gift of our lives.

Because you are the Lord of all,
yet your ears are open to our cry;
and because we delight to praise you — Father
receive the gift of our worship.

Holy, holy, holy Lord,
God of power and might,
heaven and earth are full of your glory.
Hosanna in the highest. Amen.

17 63.13★ *Doxology*

How deep the riches of the wisdom and knowledge of God!
How unsearchable his judgements,
and his paths beyond tracing out!

Who has known the mind of the Lord?
or who has been his counsellor?
Who has ever given to God,
that God should repay?

For from him and through him and to him are all things:
To God be the glory for ever! Amen.

Romans 11.33-36

Thanksgiving may be extempore, e.g:

17 63.14 We thank God for the world he has made us,
and for all his love and care:

For the warmth of the sun:
Father in heaven
we give you thanks and praise.

For the rain which makes things grow:
Father in heaven
we give you thanks and praise.

For the woods and the fields:
Father in heaven
we give you thanks and praise.

For the sea and the sky:
Father in heaven
we give you thanks and praise.

For the flowers and the animals:
Father in heaven
we give you thanks and praise.

For families and holidays:
Father in heaven
we give you thanks and praise.

For all your gifts:
Father in heaven
we give you thanks and praise.

Everything around us rejoices,
therefore give us joyful hearts
to praise you in your glory;
through Jesus Christ our Lord. Amen.

17 63.15 We give thanks to God for all his gifts to us:

For birth and life and strength of body,
for safety and shelter and food:
we give you thanks.
We praise your holy name.

For sight and hearing and the beauty of nature,
for words and music and the power of thought:
we give you thanks.
We praise your holy name.

For work and leisure and the joy of achieving,
for conscience and will and depth of feeling:
we give you thanks.
We praise your holy name.

For grace and truth in Jesus Christ,
for the gifts of the Spirit and the hope of heaven:
we give you thanks.
We praise your holy name.

We shall not forget
that you are our God,
and we are your people,
in Jesus Christ our Lord. Amen.

64 *PROPER PREFACES*

NOTE Proper Prefaces are indicated in Resource Section 8 for the Eucharistic Prayers there. These additional prefaces may be used with Rite A.

1 64.1 *Advent*

(and now we give you thanks because)
We look forward to the day when you will make
all things new
as he comes to judge the world.

1 64.2 *Advent*

And now we give you thanks
as we await the promise of salvation,
the desire of all the nations,
and the fulfilment of your good purposes
before the world began.

1 64.3 *Advent*

And now we give you thanks
because your Son our Lord was awaited by the prophets,
announced by an angel, conceived by a virgin,
and proclaimed at last to men and women of every race.

2 64.4 *Incarnation*

(and now we give you thanks because)
You shared our life in human form
from the warmth of Mary's womb to the stillness
of the grave.

2 64.5 *Incarnation*

(and now we give you thanks because)
He was born in the poverty of a stable,
to make known the riches of your kingdom.

3 64.6 *Epiphany*

(and now we give you thanks because)
You have brought us from darkness to light

and made your light shine in our hearts.
You bring us to know your glory
in the face of Jesus Christ. *2 Corinthians 4.6*

3 64.7 *Epiphany, Light*

(and now we give you thanks because)
In the wonder of the incarnation
your eternal Word has brought to the eyes of faith
a new and radiant vision of your glory.
In him we see our God made visible
and so are caught up in love of the God we cannot see.

4 64.8 *Lent, Penitence*

(and now we give you thanks because)
By his death he broke the power of sin
and made us holy through his blood.

5 64.9 *Cross*

(and now we give you thanks because)
He is the true passover lamb offered for us,
to take away the sin of the world.

5 64.10 *Cross*

(and now we give you thanks because)
For our sins he was lifted up on the cross
that he might draw the whole world to himself.

5 64.11 *Cross*

(and now we give you thanks because)
Christ is the victim who dies no more,
the Lamb, once slain, who lives for ever,
our advocate in heaven to plead our cause,
exalting us there to join the angels and archangels.

6 64.12 *Resurrection*

(and now we give you thanks because)
By his death he has destroyed death,
and by his rising again
he has restored to us eternal life.

6 64.13 *Resurrection*

(and now we give you thanks because)
By his victory over the grave
he burst the gates of death for ever.

7 64.14 *Ascension*

(and now we give you thanks because)
He humbled himself to die on a cross
but you raised him high
and gave him the name above all other names,
Jesus Christ our Lord. *Philippians 2.8,9*

8 64.15 *Pentecost*

(and now we give you thanks because)
Through him we receive the Spirit of adoption,
telling us we are your children,
and crying 'Abba, Father'. *Romans 8.15*

8 64.16 *Spirit, Pentecost*

(and now we give you thanks because)
He breathed upon his disciples the power of your Spirit
to proclaim the good news to all peoples.
John 20.21,22

8 64.17 *Baptism*

(and now we give you thanks because)
Through him we are saved for ever
and baptized into your service.

9 64.18 *Creation, Harvest*

(and now we give you thanks because)
All things are of your making,
all times and seasons obey your laws,
but you chose to create us in your own image,
setting us over the whole world in all its wonder.
You made us stewards of your creation,
to praise you day by day for the marvels of
your wisdom and power:
so earth unites with heaven
to sing the new song of creation.

9 64.19 *Bread of Life*

(and now we give you thanks because)
He broke bread with those whom others scorned
and when the multitude were hungry
he fed them abundantly.

9 64.20 *The Vine*

(and now we give you thanks because)
He is the true vine, your chosen one,
in whom we are joined to bear fruit in plenty.

10 64.21 *Word and Wisdom*

(and now we give you thanks because)
The wisdom of your word sustains all things,
and reveals you to us in your fullness.

12 64.22 *City, World and Society*

(and now we give you thanks because)
You call us to live in your city here,
while we look for the city which is to come,
designed and built by you,
with eternal foundations,
to which we journey as citizens of heaven.
Hebrews 13.14; 11.10

12 64.23 *City*

(and now we give you thanks because)
He gave up his life outside the city gate
and opened for all the way to heaven. *Hebrews 13.12*

13 64.24 *Family*

(. . .and now we give you thanks because)
A man leaves his father and mother
and is joined to his wife.
You make them one flesh.
You put us together in families,
to grasp your love and forgiveness,
care and protection, respect and authority
reflected in those around us.
And as we grow, you prepare to bring us
into the glorious freedom of your children,
as brothers and sisters of Jesus Christ.
Genesis 2.24; Romans 8.17,22

14 64.25 *Saints*

(and now we give you thanks because)
In him you have received us as your sons and daughters,
joined us in one fellowship with the saints,
and made us citizens of your kingdom.

15 64.26 *Kingdom*

(and now we give you thanks because)
He came among us as a servant,
to be Emmanuel, your presence with us.

15 64.27 *Kingdom, Ascension*

(and now we give you thanks because)
Jesus has been given all authority
in heaven and on earth,
to present to you, his Father,
a kingdom of truth, holiness and everlasting love.

16 64.28 *Marriage, Love*

(and now we give you thanks because)
In the covenant of marriage
you show us your divine love,
a mirror of your will for all creation
made new and united for ever.

17 64.29 *General*

(and now we give you thanks because)
As a mother tenderly gathers her children
you embraced a people as your own,
that with all the powers of heaven
we may find a voice to sing your praise.

NOTE These may be used as part of, or the climax to, a Word Service, or as the preface in Eucharistic Prayer D.

2 65.1 *Incarnation, Christmas, Annunciation, Mary*

Blessed are you, God of all glory,
through your Son Jesus Christ.
His name is Jesus:
Because he saves his people from their sins.

He will be called Emmanuel:
God is with us. Alleluia !

Let us praise the Lord, the God of Israel:
He has come to his people and set them free.

He gave up all the glory of heaven:
and took the nature of a servant.

In humility he walked the path of obedience:
to die on the cross.

God raised him to the highest place above
and gave him the name above every name:
Jesus Christ is Lord!

So all beings in heaven and earth will fall at his feet,
and proclaim to the glory of God:
Jesus Christ is Lord!

Today Christ is born:
Alleluia !

Today the Saviour has come:
Alleluia !

Today the angels sing on earth:
Alleluia ! Glory to God in the highest!

So, with angels and archangels,
and all the company of heaven,
we praise you for ever, saying

Holy, holy, holy Lord,
God of power and might,
heaven and earth are full of your glory.
Hosanna in the highest.

Matthew 1.21,23; Philippians 2.9-11

2 65.2 *Incarnation*

Father, we give you thanks and praise
for Jesus Christ our Lord:
he was the Word before all creation.
Through him all things come to be,
not one thing has its being but through him.

Jesus, light of the world
we worship and adore you.

Your life is the light that shines in the dark,
a light that darkness cannot overpower.

Jesus, light of the world
we worship and adore you.

The Word was the true light coming into the world.
You were in the world
that had its being through you,
and the world did not know you.

Jesus, light of the world
we worship and adore you.

You came to your own, and they did not accept you.
But to all who accept you
you give power to become children of God.

Jesus, light of the world
we worship and adore you.

The Word was made flesh and lived among us,
and we have seen his glory,
as the only Son of the Father,
full of grace and truth.

Jesus, light of the world
we worship and adore you.

So, with angels and archangels,
and all the company of heaven,
we praise the Father for ever, saying

Holy, holy, holy Lord,
God of power and might,
heaven and earth are full of your glory.
Hosanna in the highest. *John 1*

2 65.3 *Incarnation, Christmas, Annunciation, Mary*

Blessed are you, God of all glory,
through your Son Jesus Christ.

Heavenly King, born of Mary;
Jesus, Son of God
we worship and adore you.

Word of the Father, crying as a baby;
Jesus, Son of God
we worship and adore you.

Robed in glory, wrapped in infant clothes;
Jesus, Son of God
we worship and adore you.

Lord of heaven and earth, laid in a manger;
Jesus, Son of God
we worship and adore you.

To you, Jesus,
strong in your weakness,
glorious in your humility,
be all praise and glory.
We join with all the company of heaven, saying

**Holy, holy, holy Lord,
God of power and might,
heaven and earth are full of your glory.
Hosanna in the highest.**

**Blessed is he who comes in the name of the Lord.
Hosanna in the highest.**

2 65.4 *Incarnation, Christmas, Annunciation, Mary*

Blessed are you, Son of Mary;
born a child,
you share our humanity:
Heaven and earth shout their praise.

Blessed are you, Son of David;
born to rule,
you receive gifts from the wise:
Heaven and earth shout their praise.

Blessed are you, Son of Man;
born our Saviour,
you are the light of the world:
Heaven and earth shout their praise.

With all the voices of heaven
we celebrate the coming of our God:
Heaven and earth shout their praise:

Holy, holy, holy Lord,
God of power and might,
heaven and earth are full of your glory.
Hosanna in the highest.

Blessed is he who comes in the name of the Lord.
Hosanna in the highest.

3 65.5 *Lent, Penitence*

We give you thanks and praise, Father in heaven,
through Jesus Christ, your only Son, our Lord.
Through him you created the world.
Through his word the universe is sustained.

Father in heaven
we give you thanks and praise.

Through him we come near to you,
with sincere heart and sure faith.
Because of the death of Jesus
we come into the holy place.

Father in heaven
we give you thanks and praise.

He is our high priest.
He knows and feels our weaknesses.
He was tempted in every way,
like us, but did not sin.

Father in heaven
we give you thanks and praise.

By his own blood he went through the tabernacle.
He entered once and for all into the holy place.
He obtained eternal salvation for us.
he is our perfect sacrifice.

Father in heaven
we give you thanks and praise.

So we come by that living way,
the new way he opened for us,
to receive mercy and grace,
and to join with angels and archangels
and all the company of heaven, saying

**Holy, holy, holy Lord,
God of power and might,
heaven and earth are full of your glory.
Hosanna in the highest.**

Hebrews 1.3; 4.15,16; 9.12; 10.19-22

5 65.6 *Cross*

Blessed are you, God of pain and mercy,
through your Son Jesus Christ:

Surely he has borne our griefs;
he has carried our sorrows.
**Surely he has borne our griefs;
he has carried our sorrows.**

He was despised; he was rejected,
a man of sorrows and acquainted with grief:
He has carried our sorrows.

He was pierced for our sins,
bruised for no fault but ours:
He has carried our sorrows.

His punishment has bought our peace,
and by his wounds we are healed:
He has carried our sorrows.

We had all strayed like sheep,
but the Lord has laid on him the guilt of us all:
He has carried our sorrows.

Blessed are you, God of pain and mercy.
Through your Son Jesus Christ
with angels and archangels,
and all the company of heaven,
we praise you for ever, saying

**Holy, holy, holy Lord,
God of power and might,
heaven and earth are full of your glory.
Hosanna in the highest.** *Isaiah 53*

5 65.7 *Cross*

Thanks and praise be to you, almighty God.
You justify us through faith
and give us peace in our Lord Jesus Christ.

Through faith
we are saved by grace.

through him you brought us by faith
into this experience of your grace in which we now live.
And we rejoice in the hope of sharing your glory.

Through faith
we are saved by grace.

Not only so, but we also rejoice in our sufferings,
because we know that suffering produces perseverance;
perseverance, character; and character, hope.

Through faith
we are saved by grace.

And hope does not disappoint us
because you have poured out your love
into our hearts by the Holy Spirit.

Through faith
we are saved by grace.

You show us how much you love us.
While we were helpless, Christ died for the ungodly.
While we were still sinners, Christ died for us.

Through faith
we are saved by grace.

And through faith we stand in heaven and worship you
with angels and archangels, saying,

**Holy, holy, holy Lord,
God of power and might,
heaven and earth are full of your glory.
Hosanna in the highest.**

Romans 5.1-9

6 65.8 *Resurrection*

Blessed are you,
God and Father of our Lord Jesus Christ!
By your great mercy
we have been born anew to a living hope
through the resurrection of your Son from the dead,
and to an inheritance
which is imperishable,
undefiled, and unfading.
Once we were no people,
but now we are your people,
declaring your wonderful deeds in Christ,
who called us out of darkness
into his marvellous light.

By the baptism
of his death and resurrection
you gave birth to your Church,
delivered us from slavery to sin and death,
and made with us a new covenant.
At his ascension
you exalted him to sit at your right hand,
where according to his promise
he is with us always,
baptizing us with the Holy Spirit
and with fire.

The joy of resurrection fills the whole world,
and therefore we join with angels and archangels
and the whole company of heaven,
in the song of unending praise, saying

Holy, holy, holy Lord,
God of power and might,
heaven and earth are full of your glory.
Hosanna in the highest.

6 65.9 *Resurrection*

We give you thanks and praise
for the gospel we have received.
Christ died for our sins: Alleluia!
He is risen indeed. Alleluia!

He was laid in the tomb;
death could not hold him;
you raised him to life on the third day: Alleluia!
He is risen indeed. Alleluia!

Death came to all through Adam,
and sin reigned.
New life without end comes through Christ,
and he reigns for ever: Alleluia!
He is risen indeed. Alleluia!

Death, where is your victory?
Death, where is your sting?
Death is swallowed up in victory –
the victory you give us in Christ: Alleluia!
He is risen indeed. Alleluia!

We have been crucified with Christ,
and live his risen life,
to praise you for ever with angels and archangels:

Holy, holy, holy Lord,
God of power and might,
heaven and earth are full of your glory.
Hosanna in the highest.

1 Corinthians 15

7 65.10 *Ascension, Kingship*

Thanks and praise be to you, Lord of heaven,
for Jesus Christ your Son our Lord.
You gave him the name above every name,
so that we say,

Jesus, Lord of all
we worship and adore you.

King of righteousness, King of peace,
enthroned at the right hand of Majesty on high:
Jesus, Lord of all
we worship and adore you.

Great high priest, living for ever to intercede for us:
Jesus, Lord of all
we worship and adore you.

Pioneer of our salvation, you bring us to glory
through your death and resurrection:

Jesus, Lord of all

We worship and adore you.
Every knee bows to you;
every tongue confesses: you are Lord,
to the glory of God the Father.
Blessed is he who comes in the name of the Lord.
Hosanna in the highest.

7 65.11 *Ascension, Kingship*

Father, we are in your Spirit and we hear your voice:
'I am the first and the last, who is, who was,
and who is to come.'
Before the worlds were made, Christ was alive.
Through him you created everything in heaven
and on earth,
the seen and the unseen, spiritual powers,
lords and authorities,
the whole universe created through him and for him:

Lord of glory
we worship and adore you.

You sent him, the visible likeness
of the invisible God,
to reflect the brightness of your glory,
to sustain the universe with his word of power,
to achieve forgiveness for the sins of all.

Lord of glory
we worship and adore you.

And now he rules in heaven, mighty risen Lord,
his hair as white as snow, his eyes like fire,
his feet like polished brass, his hands full of stars,
his face bright as the noonday sun,
his voice like a roaring waterfall:
'I am the living one!
I was dead but now I am alive for ever and ever.'

Lord of glory
we worship and adore you.

So, with angels and archangels,
and all the company of heaven,
we praise you for ever, saying

Holy, holy, holy Lord,
God of power and might,
heaven and earth are full of your glory.
Hosanna in the highest.

Colossians 1.15-20;
Hebrews 1.3; Revelation 1.14-18

The acclamation may be repeated between each line of the last paragraph.

8 65.12 *Spirit, Pentecost, Gifts, Healing,*
Baptism and Confirmation

All of your creation groans with pain
like the pain of childbirth,
and longs to share the freedom of the children of God.
Your Spirit pleads for us
in groans words cannot express.

Father in heaven
we give you thanks and praise.

The law of the Spirit brings us life in Christ,
and sets us free from the law of sin and death.

Father in heaven
we give you thanks and praise.

Like all who are led by your Spirit,
we are your children.
By your Spirit's power we cry 'Abba, Father'.

Father in heaven
we give you thanks and praise.

The Spirit confirms that we are your children.
And if children, then we are heirs,
fellow-heirs with Christ, sharing his suffering now
that we may share his glory.

Father in heaven
we give you thanks and praise.

So by your Spirit we praise you for ever
and proclaim your glory with all the company
of heaven, saying

Holy, holy, holy Lord,
God of power and might,
heaven and earth are full of your glory.
Hosanna in the highest.

Romans 8.2,14-25

8 65.13 *Spirit, Baptism and Confirmation*

(This section is not to be used with Eucharistic Prayer D)

Father, for your gift of water in creation:
we give you thanks and praise.

For your Spirit, sweeping over the waters,
bringing light and life:
we give you thanks and praise.

For your Son Jesus Christ our Lord,
baptized in the river Jordan:
we give you thanks and praise.

For your new creation,
brought to birth by water and the Spirit:
we give you thanks and praise.

For your grace bestowed upon us your children,
washing away our sins:
we give you thanks and praise.

So, Father, accept our sacrifice of praise;
By the power of your life-giving Spirit
bless these waters of your new creation:
Lord, receive our prayer.

May your servants who are washed in them
be made one with your Son,
who took the form of a servant:
Lord, receive our prayer.

May your Holy Spirit bring them to new birth
in the family of your Church,
and raise them in Christ, our anointed Lord,
to full and eternal life:
Lord, receive our prayer.

For all might, majesty and dominion are yours,
now and for ever. **Alleluia ! Amen.**

9 65.14 *Creation*

You are the image of the unseen God,
the first-born of all creation.
You created all things in heaven and on earth:
everything visible and everything invisible,
thrones, dominions, sovereignties, powers -
all things were created through you and for you.

Lord of all creation
we worship and adore you.

You are the radiant light of God's glory:
You hold all creation together by your word of power.

Lord of all creation
we worship and adore you.

As you are the beginning,
you were first to be born from the dead.
all perfection was found in you,
and all things were reconciled through you and for you,
everything in heaven and everything on earth,
when you made peace by your death on the cross.

Lord of all creation
we worship and adore you.

The Church is your body,
you are its head.
You take your place in heaven
at the right hand of the divine majesty.

Lord of all creation
we worship and adore you.

Holy, holy, holy Lord,
God of power and might,
heaven and earth are full of your glory.
Hosanna in the highest.

Blessed is he who comes in the name of the Lord.
Hosanna in the highest.

Colossians 1.15-18

12 65.15 *City, World and Society*

Father, you gave up your Son for us all:
you give us all things with him;
you call us, justify us, glorify us:

Father in heaven
we give you thanks and praise.

Jesus Christ died, was raised to life,
and pleads for us at your right hand.
Who can separate us from your love?

Father in heaven
we give you thanks and praise.

For your sake we face death all day long.
In your world we face trouble and hardship,
persecution, famine, nakedness, danger and death.

Father in heaven
we give you thanks and praise.

But nothing separates us from your love,
neither death nor life,
neither angels nor demons,
neither the present nor the future,
nor any heavenly powers,
neither the world above nor the world below:
nothing in all creation can separate us
from your love in Jesus Christ.

Father in heaven
we give you thanks and praise.

In all these things we are more than conquerors
through him who loves us,
and has freed us from our sins
and made us a kingdom and priests
to serve you for ever,
with all the company of heaven, saying

Holy, holy, holy Lord,
God of power and might,
heaven and earth are full of your glory.
Hosanna in the highest.

Romans 8.23-39

14 65.16 *Saints*

Blessed are you, gracious God,
creator of heaven and earth;
in the multitude of your saints
you have surrounded us with a great cloud of witnesses.

The glorious company of apostles praise you.
The noble fellowship of prophets praise you.
The white-robed army of martyrs praise you.
We your holy Church acclaim you.
In communion with angels and archangels,
and with all those who have served you in every age,
and worship you now in heaven,
we raise our voices to proclaim your glory,
for ever praising you and saying

Holy, holy, holy Lord
God of power and might,
heaven and earth are full of your glory.
Hosanna in the highest.

15 65.17 *Reconciliation*

Almighty God, creator of the world
  and everything in it,
Lord of heaven and earth,
you made the whole human race.
You have shown to us in Christ the mystery
  of your purpose:
You chose us all in Christ to praise his glory.

You will bring all things together under Christ,
all things in heaven, all things on earth,
under him as head:
You chose us all in Christ to praise his glory.

We have heard the word of truth, the good news
  of salvation,
You have stamped us with the seal of your
  Spirit of promise:
You chose us all in Christ to praise his glory.

We who once were far away
have been brought near by the blood of Christ:
You chose us all in Christ to praise his glory.

He is the peace between us,
and has broken down the barrier of hostility.
He has made us one new humanity
and reconciled us to you by the cross:
You chose us all in Christ to praise his glory.

He killed hostility and brought peace,
peace to all near at hand, peace to all far away:
You chose us all in Christ to praise his glory.

Through him we come, by the Spirit,
to you, our Father in heaven, singing

Holy, holy, holy Lord,
God of power and might,
heaven and earth are full of your glory.
Hosanna in the highest.

Acts 17.25,26; Ephesians 1.9-13; 2.13-17

17 65.18 *General*

Father, we give you thanks and praise
through Jesus Christ your Son, our Lord.

Jesus is Lord of all creation.
We worship and adore you.

1 Jesus left the glory of heaven.
We worship and adore you.

2 Jesus died to set us free.
We worship and adore you.

3 Jesus was raised to life again.
We worship and adore you.

4 Jesus reigns in glory now.
We worship and adore you.

5 We worship and adore you with angels and archangels
and all the company of heaven, saying
Holy, holy, holy Lord,
God of power and might,
heaven and earth are full of your glory.
Hosanna in the highest.

This anthem may also be used

Blessed is he who comes in the name of the Lord.
Hosanna in the highest.

Insertions: the following seasonal and other sentences may be inserted at the points indicated. Not all need be used, and a selection should certainly be made from sections 4 and 5. The response to each is

We worship and adore you.

1 Jesus, born of the Virgin Mary:
Jesus, cradled in a manger:
Jesus, Saviour, Christ our Lord:
Jesus, God in human flesh:
Jesus our Emmanuel:

2 Jesus lifted up for us:
Jesus stretches out his arms:
Jesus died for a dying world:
Jesus bore our sins and griefs:

3 Jesus lay within the tomb:
Jesus rose to life in triumph:
Jesus conquers death for us:

4 Jesus, Lord of life and death:
Jesus, Lamb upon the throne:
Jesus crowned, in glory seated:
Jesus, always pleading for us:
Jesus comes again in glory:
Jesus claims his kingdom here:

5 Jesus is the Son of God:
Jesus is the light of the world:
Jesus is the bread of heaven:
Jesus, our way, our truth, our life:
Jesus is the door to life:
Jesus is the first and last:
Jesus is the Lord of all:
Jesus our wisdom from above:
Jesus is the King of Kings:
Jesus is our friend and brother:
Jesus, healer of the sick:
Alleluia! Praise the Lord!

NOTES

a It is not necessary always to end each song with 'Glory to the Father . . .'. It may be omitted as required.

b A song may be said responsively with the suggested response after each verse or pair of verses. Alternatively, a song may be said, or sung, by all the worshippers, either together or responsively by half verses or verses.

c An alternative method of saying or singing a song would be the use of a metrical version.

1 66.1 *Advent*

A SONG OF THE WILDERNESS

Response **The ransomed of the Lord shall return with singing.**

1 The wilderness and the dry land shall rejoice:
the desert shall burst into song.

2 They shall see the glory of the Lord:
the splendour of our God.

3 Strengthen the weary hands:
make firm the feeble knees.

4 Say to the anxious, be strong, fear not:
your God is coming in judgement to save you.

5 Then shall the eyes of the blind be opened:
and the ears of the deaf unstopped;

6 Then the lame shall leap like the deer:
and the tongue of the dumb sing for joy.

7 For waters shall spring up in the wilderness:
and streams flow in the desert.

8 The ransomed of the Lord shall return with singing:
crowned with everlasting joy.

9 They shall obtain joy and gladness:
and sorrow and sighing shall flee away.

Glory to the Father, and to the Son:
and to the Holy Spirit;
as it was in the beginning, is now:
and shall be for ever. Amen.

Isaiah 35.1 - 6.10

1 66.2 *Advent*

A SONG OF THE BRIDE

Response **He has clothed me with the garments of salvation.**

1 I will greatly rejoice in the Lord:
my soul shall exult in my God.

2 For he has clothed me with the garments of salvation:
he has covered me with the cloak of integrity.

3 As a bridegroom decks himself with a garland:
and as a bride adorns herself with her jewels.

4 For as the earth puts forth her blossom:
and as seeds in the garden spring up.

5 So shall the Lord God make righteousness and praise:
blossom before all the nations.

6 For Zion's sake, I will not keep silence:
and for Jerusalem's sake, I will not rest.

7 Until her deliverance shines forth like the sunrise:
and her salvation as a burning torch.

8 The nations shall see your deliverance:
and all kings shall see your glory.

9 Then you shall be called by a new name:
which the mouth of the Lord will give.

10 You shall be a crown of glory in the hand of the Lord:
and a royal diadem in the hand of your God.

Glory to the Father, and to the Son:
and to the Holy Spirit;
as it was in the beginning, is now:
and shall be for ever. Amen.

Isaiah 61.10-11 and 62.1-3

2 66.3 *Incarnation, Christmas, Annunciation, Mary*

A SONG OF JOY

Response **To us a child is born, to us a son is given.**

1 The people who walked in darkness have seen a great light:
Those who dwelt in a land of deep darkness, upon them the light has dawned.

2 You have increased their joy and given them great gladness:
they rejoiced before you as with joy at the harvest.

3 For you have shattered the yoke which burdened them:
the collar that lay heavy upon their shoulders.

4 For to us a child is born, to us a son is given:
and the government will be upon his shoulder.

5 And his name will be called 'Wonderful Counsellor, the Mighty God:
the everlasting Father, the Prince of Peace'.

6 Of the increase of his government and of peace:
there will be no end.

7 Upon the throne of David, and over his kingdom:
to establish and uphold it with justice and righteousness.

8 From this time forth and for evermore:
the zeal of the Lord of Hosts will do this.

Glory to the Father, and to the Son:
and to the Holy Spirit;
as it was in the beginning, is now:
and shall be for ever. Amen. *Isaiah 9.2-7 adapted*

2 66.4 *Incarnation, Christmas, Annunciation, Mary*

A SONG OF PROPHECY

Response **The Spirit of the Lord shall rest upon him.**

1 There shall come forth a shoot from the stump of Jesse:
and a branch shall grow out of its roots,

2 and the Spirit of the Lord shall rest upon him:
the spirit of wisdom and understanding,

3 the spirit of counsel and might:
the spirit of knowledge and the fear of the Lord.

4 He shall not judge by what his eyes see:
or decide by what his ears hear,

5 but with righteousness he shall judge the poor:
and decide with equity for the meek of the earth.

6 The wolf shall dwell with the lamb:
and the leopard shall lie down with the kid,

7 the calf and the young lion together:
with a little child to lead them.

Glory to the Father, and to the Son:
and to the Holy Spirit;
as it was in the beginning, is now:
and shall be for ever. Amen. *Isaiah 11.1-4,6*

3 66.5 *Epiphany, Light*

A SONG OF THE NEW JERUSALEM

Response **Arise, shine out, for your light has come.**

1 Arise, shine out, for your light has come:
the glory of the Lord is rising upon you.

2 Though night still covers the earth:
and darkness the peoples,

3 Above you the Lord now rises:
and above you his glory appears.

4 The nations will come to your light:
and kings to your dawning brightness.

5 Your gates will always stand open:
shut neither by day nor by night.

6 They will call you 'The City of the Lord':
'Zion of the Holy One of Israel'.

7 The sound of violence shall be heard no longer
in your land:
or ruin and destruction within your borders.

8 You will call your walls 'Salvation':
and your gates, 'Praise'.

9 No more will the sun give you daylight:
nor the moonlight shine upon you.

10 But the Lord will be your everlasting light:
your God will be your splendour.

Glory to the Father, and to the Son:
and to the Holy Spirit;
as it was in the beginning, is now:
and shall be for ever. Amen.

Isaiah 60.1-3,11,14,18-19

3 66.6 *Epiphany, Light*

A SONG OF RESTORATION

Response **I, the Lord, will comfort my people.**

1 Listen to me, you islands:
and people who live far away.

2 My servant, in the time of my favour I will answer you:
and in the day of salvation I will help you;

3 I will restore the land:
and share out afresh its desolate fields;

4 I will say to the prisoners, 'Go free':
and to those in darkness, 'Come out to the light'.

5 They will feed beside the way:
and find pasture on every barren hill.

6 They will never hunger nor thirst:
sun and desert heat will never plague them,

7 for he who loves them will guide them:
and lead them beside springs of water.

8 Shout for joy, you heavens and exult, you earth:
mountains, break into song;

9 for I the Lord will comfort my people:
and will have compassion on my own in their distress.

Glory to the Father, and to the Son:
and to the Holy Spirit;
as it was in the beginning, is now:
and shall be for ever. Amen. *Isaiah 49:1,8-10,13*

4 66.7 *Lent, Penitence*

A SONG OF HOSEA

Response **Come let us return to the Lord.**

1 Come let us return to the Lord:
for he has torn us and will heal us.

2 He has stricken us:
and he will bind up our wounds.

3 After two days, he will revive us:
on the third day he will raise us up,
that we may live in his presence.

4 Let us humble ourselves, let us strive to know the Lord:
for his justice dawns like the morning light,
and its dawning is as sure as the sunrise.

5 He will come to us like the showers:
like the spring rains that water the earth.

6 Ephraim, how shall I deal with you?:
How shall I deal with you, Judah?

7 Your love for me is like the morning mist:
like the dew that vanishes early.

8 Therefore I have cut them in pieces by the prophets:
and my judgement goes forth as the light.

9 For loyalty is my desire, and not sacrifice:
and the knowledge of God rather than burnt offerings.

Glory to the Father, and to the Son:
and to the Holy Spirit;
as it was in the beginning, is now:
and shall be for ever. Amen. *Hosea 6.1-6*

5 66.8 *Cross*

A SONG OF THE SERVANT

Response **By his wounds we are healed.**

1 He was despised; he was rejected:
a man of sorrows, acquainted with grief.

2 As one from whom people hide their faces:
he was despised, and we did not esteem him.

3 He bore our sufferings:
he endured our torments,

4 while we thought he was being punished:
and struck by God, brought low.

5 He was pierced for our sins:
bruised for no fault but our own.

6 His punishment has won our peace:
and by his wounds we are healed.

7 We have all strayed like sheep:
each taking their own way;

8 but the Lord has laid on him:
the guilt of us all.

Glory to the Father, and to the Son:
and to the Holy Spirit;
as it was in the beginning, is now:
and shall be for ever. Amen. *Isaiah 53.3-6*

6 66.9 *Resurrection, Heaven, Glory, Transfiguration, Death, Funerals*

THE SONG OF MOSES

Response **The Lord is my strength and my song.**

1 I will sing to the Lord,
for he has triumphed gloriously:
he has thrown the horse and its rider into the sea.

2 The Lord is my strength and my song:
and he has become my salvation.

3 This is my God, and I will praise him:
the God of my father and I will exalt him.

4 Lord, who among the gods is like you:
majestic in holiness and working wonders?

6 In your unfailing love you will lead
the people you have redeemed:
in your strength you will guide them
to your holy dwelling.

7 You will bring them in and plant them on
your mountain:
the place you have made for your dwelling.

8 In the sanctuary that your hands have established:
you, Lord, will reign for ever and ever.

Glory to the Father, and to the Son:
and to the Holy Spirit;
as it was in the beginning, is now:
and shall be for ever. Amen.

Exodus 15.1,2,11,13,17

6 66.10 *Resurrection, Heaven, Glory, Transfiguration, Death, Funerals*

A SONG OF PETER

Response **Praise be to the God and Father of our Lord Jesus Christ.**

1 Praise be to the God and Father of our Lord Jesus Christ:
who in his great mercy gave you new birth as
his children.

2 He has raised Jesus Christ from the dead:
so that you have a sure hope in him.

3 You have the promise of an inheritance that can never
be spoilt:
because it is kept for you in heaven.

4 The ransom that was paid to free you:
was not paid in silver or gold;

5 but in the precious blood of Christ:
the Lamb without spot or stain.

6 God raised him from the dead and gave him glory:
so that you would have faith and hope in God.

Glory to the Father, and to the Son:
and to the Holy Spirit;
as it was in the beginning, is now:
and shall be for ever. Amen. *1 Peter 1.3-4,18-21*

8 66.11 *Spirit, Pentecost, Gifts, Healing, Baptism and Confirmation*

A SONG OF HOPE

Response **I will greatly rejoice in the Lord.**

1 The Spirit of the Lord God is upon me:
because the Lord has anointed me
to bring good tidings to the afflicted.

2 The Lord has sent me to bind up the broken-hearted:
to proclaim liberty for the captives,
and release for those in prison,

3 to comfort all who mourn:
to bestow on them a crown of beauty instead of ashes,

4 the oil of gladness instead of mourning:
a garment of splendour for the heavy heart.

5 They shall be called trees of righteousness:
planted for the glory of the Lord.

6 Therefore I will greatly rejoice in the Lord:
my soul shall exult in my God,

7 for God has robed me with salvation as a garment:
and clothed me with integrity as a cloak.

8 For as the earth brings forth its shoots:
and as a garden causes the seeds to spring up,

9 so the Lord God will cause righteousness and praise:
to spring forth before all the nations.

Glory to the Father, and to the Son:
and to the Holy Spirit;
as it was in the beginning, is now:
and shall be for ever. Amen. *Isaiah 61.1-3,10,11*

9 66.12 *Creation, Harvest, Bread, Word*
(especially suitable for use at the Eucharist)

A SONG OF THE BREAD OF HEAVEN

Response **Jesus Christ is the bread of heaven.**

1 You gave your people the food of angels:
and sent them bread from heaven.

2 It was ready to eat, though they did no work:
it was rich in delights, suiting every taste.

3 The food which you gave:
showed your sweetness toward your children.

4 It satisfied the desire of those who ate:
and was flavoured as each one wished;

5 That the children you love might learn, Lord God:
that they are not fed by various crops.

6 It is your word which sustains:
all those who trust in you.

Glory to the Father, and to the Son:
and to the Holy Spirit;
as it was in the beginning, is now:
and shall be for ever. Amen. *Wisdom 16.20-21,26*

10 66.13 *Word*

A SONG OF THE WORD

Response **Seek the Lord while he may be found.**

1 Seek the Lord while he may be found:
call on him while he is near.

2 Let the wicked abandon their ways:
and the unrighteous their thoughts.

3 Turn back to the Lord, who will have mercy:
to our God, who will richly pardon.

4 'For my thoughts are not your thoughts:
neither are your ways my ways,' says the Lord.

5 'As the heavens are higher than the earth:
so are my ways higher than your ways
and my thoughts than your thoughts.

6 As the rain and snow come down from heaven:
and return not again but water the earth,

7 bringing forth life and giving growth:
seed for sowing and bread to eat,

8 so is my word that goes out from my mouth:
it does not return to me empty,

9 but it will accomplish my purpose:
and succeed in the task I give it.'

Glory to the Father, and to the Son:
and to the Holy Spirit;
as it was in the beginning, is now:
and shall be for ever. Amen.

Isaiah 55.6-11

11 66.14 *Mission, Unity, Kingdom*

A SONG OF A HERALD

Response **Lift up your voice with strength**

1 Go up to a high mountain,
herald of good tidings to Zion:
lift up your voice with strength,
herald of good tidings to Jerusalem.

2 Lift it up, fear not:
say to the cities of Judah, 'Behold your God.'

3 See the Lord coming with might:
coming to rule with his mighty arm.

4 He brings his reward with him:
his recompense before him.

5 He will feed his flock like a shepherd:
and gather the lambs in his arms.

6 He will hold them to his breast:
and gently lead those with young.

Glory to the Father, and to the Son:
and to the Holy Spirit;
as it was in the beginning, is now:
and shall be for ever. Amen.

Isaiah 40.9-11

12 66.15 *City, World and Society*
(also suitable for Advent)

A SONG OF THE HOLY CITY

Response **Behold, I make all things new.**

1 I saw a new heaven and a new earth:
for the first heaven and the first earth had passed away
and there was no longer any sea.

2 I saw the holy city, new Jerusalem,
coming down out of heaven from God:
prepared as a bride adorned for her husband.

3 I heard a great voice from the throne saying:
'Behold, the dwelling place of God is with people.

4 He will wipe away every tear from their eyes:
and God himself will be with them.

5 He will wipe away every tear from their eyes:
and death shall be no more.

6 There shall be no mourning
nor crying, nor pain any more:
for the former things have passed away.'

7 And he who sat upon the throne said:
'Behold, I make all things new.'

Glory to the Father, and to the Son:
and to the Holy Spirit;
as it was in the beginning, is now:
and shall be for ever. Amen. *Revelation 21.1-5a*

14 66.16 *Saints*

A SONG OF WISDOM

Response **Glory to the one who gives me wisdom.**

1 Wisdom freed a holy people and a blameless race:
from a nation of oppressors.

2 She entered the soul of a servant of the Lord:
and withstood fearsome rulers with wonders
and signs.

3 To the saints she gave the reward of their labours:
and led them by a marvellous road;

4 She was their shelter by day:
and a blaze of stars by night.

5 She brought them across the Red Sea:
she led them through mighty waters.

6 She swallowed their enemies in the waves:
and spat them out from the depths of the sea.

7 Then, Lord, the righteous sang the glories of your name:
and praised together your protecting hand;

8 For wisdom opened the mouths of the silent:
and gave speech to the tongues of her children.

Glory to the Father, and to the Son:
and to the Holy Spirit;
as it was in the beginning, is now:
and shall be for ever. Amen. *Wisdom 10.15-19,20b-21*

15 66.17 *Kingdom, Freedom, Reconciliation*

THE SONG OF HANNAH

Response **My heart rejoices in the Lord.**

1 My heart rejoices in the Lord:
my strength is exalted in my God.

2 There is no one holy like the Lord:
there is no one like you, no rock like our God.

3 For you Lord are a God who knows:
and by you our actions are weighed.

4 The bows of the mighty are broken:
but the feeble gird on strength.

5 You Lord make poor and make rich:
you bring low and you also exalt.

6 You raise up the poor from the dust:
and lift the needy from the ash-heap.

7 You make them sit with princes:
and inherit a seat of honour.

8 For the foundations of the earth are yours, Lord:
and on them you have set the world.

Glory to the Father, and to the Son:
and to the Holy Spirit;
as it was in the beginning, is now:
and shall be for ever. Amen. *1 Samuel 2.1-4,7,8*

15 66.18 *Kingdom, Freedom, Reconciliation*

A SONG OF SALVATION

Response: **I will trust and will not be afraid.**

1 Behold God is my salvation:
I will trust and will not be afraid.

2 For the Lord God is my strength and my song:
and he has become my salvation.

3 With joy you will draw water:
from the wells of salvation.

4 On that day you will say:
'Give thanks to the Lord, call upon his name.

5 Make known his deeds among the nations:
proclaim that his name is exalted.

6 Sing praises to the Lord, for he has triumphed gloriously:
let this be known in all the earth.

7 Shout and sing for joy, you that dwell in Zion:
for great in your midst is the Holy One of Israel.'

Glory to the Father, and to the Son:
and to the Holy Spirit;
as it was in the beginning is now:
and shall be for ever. Amen. *Isaiah 12.2-6*

16 66.19 *Peace*

A SONG OF PEACE

Response **Let us walk in the light of the Lord.**

1 'Let us go up to the Mountain of the Lord,
to the house of the God of Jacob,

2 That he may teach us his ways:
that we may walk in his paths.'

3 For the law shall go out from Zion:
and the word of the Lord from Jerusalem.

4 He shall judge between the nations:
and settle disputes for many peoples.

5 They shall beat their swords into ploughshares:
their spears into pruning hooks.

6 Nation shall not lift up sword against nation:
nor ever again be trained for war.

7 People of Jacob, come:
let us walk in the light of the Lord.

Glory to the Father, and to the Son:
and to the Holy Spirit;
as it was in the beginning, is now:
and shall be for ever. Amen. *Isaiah 2.2-5*

16 66.20 *Love, Peace*

THE PROMISE OF THE NEW JERUSALEM

Response **Rejoice with Jerusalem and exult in her.**

1 Rejoice with Jerusalem and exult in her:
all you who love her;

2 share her joy with all your heart:
all you who mourn over her.

3 Then you may suck and be fed from her breasts:
delighting in her plentiful milk.

4 For thus says the Lord,
I will send peace flowing over her like a river:
and the wealth of nations like a stream in flood;

5 Jerusalem shall suckle you:
and you shall be carried in her arms
and rocked upon her knees.

6 As a mother comforts her child:
so will I myself comfort you,
and you shall find strength in Jerusalem.

7 This you shall see and be glad at heart:
your limbs shall be as the fresh grass in spring;

8 Then I myself will gather all nations:
and they shall come and behold my glory.

Glory to the Father, and to the Son:
and to the Holy Spirit;
as it was in the beginning, is now:
and shall be for ever. Amen. *Isaiah 66.10-14a,18b*

16 66.21 *Love, Peace*

A SONG OF GOD'S LOVE

Response **Let us love one another, for love is from God.**

1 Let us love one another:
for love is from God.

2 Those who love are born of God and know God:
but those who do not love
know nothing of God; for God is love.

3 Those who dwell in love:
are dwelling in God and God in them.

4 There is no room for fear in love:
love which is perfected banishes fear.

5 We love because God first loved us:
If anyone who hates another says, 'I love God',
that person is a liar.

6 If we do not love those whom we have seen:
we cannot love God whom we have not seen.

7 This commandment we have from God:
that those who love God must also love
their neighbour.

Glory to the Father, and to the Son:
and to the Holy Spirit;
as it was in the beginning, is now:
and shall be for ever. Amen. *1 John 4.7,8,16,18-21*

17 66.22 *General*

THE BEATITUDES

Response **Rejoice and be glad, for your reward is great in heaven.**

1 Blessed are the poor in spirit:
for theirs is the kingdom of heaven.

2 Blessed are those who mourn:
for they shall be comforted.

3 Blessed are the gentle:
for they shall inherit the earth.

4 Blessed are those who hunger and thirst for what is right:
for they shall be satisfied.

5 Blessed are the merciful:
for mercy shall be shown to them.

6 Blessed are the pure in heart:
for they shall see God.

7 Blessed are the peacemakers:
for they shall be called children of God.

8 Blessed are those who are persecuted in the cause of right:
for theirs is the kingdom of heaven.

9 Blessed are you when others revile you and persecute you:
and utter all kinds of evil against you falsely for my sake.

10 Rejoice and be glad:
for your reward is great in heaven.

(Glory to the Father, and to the Son:
and to the Holy Spirit;
as it was in the beginning, is now:
and shall be for ever. Amen.)

Matthew 5.3-12

17 66.23 *General*

A SONG OF SALVATION

Response **Blessed be the God and Father of our Lord Jesus Christ.**

1 Blessed are you, God and Father of our Lord
Jesus Christ:
you have blessed us in Christ
with all the spiritual blessings of heaven.

2 Even before the world was made
you chose us to be yours in Christ:
to be holy and without blame.

3 In love you planned to adopt us
as your children through Jesus Christ:

4 that we might praise your glorious grace:
your free gift to us in your beloved Son.

5 In Christ we gain redemption:
through his blood our sins are forgiven;
how rich is your grace!

Glory to the Father, and to the Son:
and to the Holy Spirit;
as it was in the beginning, is now:
and shall be for ever. Amen. *Ephesians 1.3-7*

17 66.24 *General*

A SONG OF ANSELM

Responses
either **Jesus, as a mother you gather your people to you.**
or **In your love and tenderness remake us.**

1 Jesus, as a mother you gather your people to you:
you are gentle with us as a mother with her children;

2 Often you weep over our sins and our pride:
tenderly you draw us from hatred and judgement.

3 You comfort us in sorrow and bind up our wounds:
in sickness you nurse us, and with pure milk you
feed us.

4 Jesus, by your dying we are born to new life:
by your anguish and labour we come forth in joy.

5 Despair turns to hope through your sweet goodness:
through your gentleness we find comfort in fear.

6 Your warmth gives life to the dead:
your touch makes sinners righteous.

7 Lord Jesus, in your mercy heal us:
in your love and tenderness remake us;

8 In your compassion bring grace and forgiveness:
for the beauty of heaven may your love prepare us.

17 66.25 *General*

A SONG OF PILGRIMAGE

Response **Glory to the one who gives me wisdom!**

1 While I was still young, before I began my travels:
I sought for wisdom openly in my prayers.

2 I asked for her outside the temple sanctuary:
and I will seek her to the end.

3 She has been the delight of my heart:
from first blossom to early fruit.

4 I have kept firmly to the true path:
I have followed her steps since my youth.

5 I bowed my ear a little and received her:
I found wisdom and was well instructed.

6 Glory to the one who gives me wisdom!
I will live according to her way.

7 From the beginning I gained understanding from her:
therefore I will never be deserted.

8 Because I longed to find her with all my heart:
I have gained a good possession.

9 As my reward the Lord has given me a tongue:
with which I shall sing his praises.

Glory to the Father, and to the Son:
and to the Holy Spirit;
as it was in the beginning, is now:
and shall be for ever. Amen.

Ecclesiasticus 51.13-18a,20b-22

7 INTRODUCTORY WORDS

71 *INTRODUCTORY WORDS TO THE PEACE*

Note 20 in Rite A Holy Communion provides for the Peace to be used at other points than the one provided. It can profitably be used at the beginning of the service, or at the end of Communion or Family Service. Section 30 in Rite A provides for other suitable words to be used instead of those in the service; some are provided at section 83 of the service, and more here. The pattern is easy to copy, for instance to provide words for special occasions or to echo some particular teaching in the sermon. The introductory words should not be a prayer, but an encouragement, based on Scripture, to minister peace to one another. The second sentence, 'The peace of the Lord be always with you' is best kept as a standard introduction to the response, but may be seasonally varied, as for example, 'The peace of the risen Lord be always with you.'

1 71.1 *Advent*

In the tender compassion of our God
the dawn from on high shall break upon us,
to shine on those who dwell in darkness and the shadow of death,
and to guide our feet into the way of peace.
The peace of the Lord be always with you. . .

Luke 1.78-79

1 71.2 *Advent*

The God of peace makes us holy in all things
that we may be ready at the coming of our Lord Jesus Christ.
The peace of the Lord be always with you. . .

1 Thess. 5.23

2 71.3 *Incarnation, Christmas*

Glory to God in the highest,
and on earth peace to all on whom his favour rests.
The peace of the Lord be always with you. . .

Luke 2.14

3 71.4 *Epiphany*

Sovereign Lord, your word has been fulfilled;
my eyes have seen your salvation:
now you let your servant go in peace.
The peace of the Lord be always with you. . .

Luke 2.29

5 71.5 *Cross*

Now that we have been put right with God
through faith,
we have peace with God through our Lord Jesus Christ.
The peace of the Lord be always with you. . .

Romans 5.1

5 71.6 *Cross*

Now in union with Christ Jesus
you who once were far off
have been brought near
through the shedding of Christ's blood;
for he is our peace.
The peace of the Lord be always with you. . .

Ephesians 2.13

8 71.7 *Spirit, Pentecost, Gifts, Healing, Baptism and Confirmation*

We are baptized into Christ:
live in the Spirit of Christ.
The peace of the Lord be always with you. . .

8 71.8 *Spirit, Pentecost, Gifts, Healing, Baptism and Confirmation*

The mind of sinful nature is death;
The mind controlled by the Spirit is life and peace.
The peace of the Lord be always with you. . .

Romans 8.6

8 71.9 *Trinity*

Peace to you from God our heavenly Father.
Peace from his Son Jesus Christ who is our peace.
Peace from the Holy Spirit the lifegiver.
The peace of the triune God be always with you. . .

9 71.10 *Harvest*

Peacemakers who sow in peace raise a harvest of righteousness.
The peace of the Lord be always with you. . .

James 3.18

11 71.11 *Church, Mission and Ministry, Unity*

We are the body of Christ.
By one Spirit we were baptized into one body.
Keep the unity of the Spirit in the bond of peace.
We are bound by the love of Christ.
The peace of the Lord be always with you. . .

1 Corinthians 12.13

11 71.12 *Church, Mission and Ministry, Unity*

We are all one in Christ Jesus.
We belong to him through faith,
heirs of the promise of the Spirit of peace.
The peace of the Lord be always with you . . .

Galatians 3.28

13 71.13 *Family*

Jesus said, 'Whoever does the will of God is my brother, and sister and mother'.
As we have opportunity, let us work for good to all, especially members of the household of faith.
The peace of the Lord be always with you . . .

15 71.14 *Kingdom, Freedom, Reconciliation*

God calls us to peace:
In God's justice is our peace.
Christ calls us to be God's people:
In Christ is our peace.
The peace of the Lord be always with you . . .

Ephesians 2.14-15

15 71.15 *Kingdom, Freedom, Reconciliation*

Blessed be Christ, the prince of peace.
He breaks down the walls that divide us:
Praise Christ who is our peace!
The peace of the Lord be always with you . . .

15 71.16 *Kingdom, Freedom, Reconciliation*

God has reconciled us to himself through Christ
and given us the ministry of reconciliation.
The peace of the Lord be always with you . . .
2 Corinthians 5.18

16 71.17 *Love, Peace*

Love one another;
as I have loved you,
so you are to love one another.
The peace of the Lord be always with you . . .
John 15.12

16 71.18 *Wedding*

We have celebrated the love of *N* and *N*.
We now celebrate God's love for all of us.
Greet one another with a kiss of love.
Peace in Christ to all of you . . .
1 Peter 5.14

16 71.19 *Love, Peace*

Let love be genuine. Never pay back evil for evil.
As far as it lies with you, live at peace with everyone.
The peace of the Lord be always with you . . .
Romans 12.9,17,18

16 71.20 *Love, Unity*

To crown all things there must be love,
to bind all together and complete the whole.
Let the peace of Christ rule in your hearts.
The peace of the Lord be always with you . . .
Colossians 3.14

17 71.21 *General, Memorials and in Time of Trouble*

Jesus says to his disciples,
Peace I leave with you; my peace I give you.
I do not give to you as the world gives.
Let not your hearts be troubled or afraid.
The peace of the Lord be always with you . . .
John 14.27

17 71.22 *General*

Blessed are those who make peace:
they shall be called sons and daughters of God.
We meet in the name of Christ and share his peace.
The peace of the Lord be always with you . . .

Matthew 5.9

17 71.23 *General*

God will speak peace to his people,
to those who turn to him in their hearts.
The peace of the Lord be always with you . . .

1 Samuel 12.22

17 71.24 *At an Agape*

The kingdom of God is not a matter of eating and drinking,
but of righteousness, peace and joy in the Holy Spirit.
The peace of the Lord be always with you . . .

Romans 14.17

17 71.25 *General*

God has called us to live in peace.
The peace of the Lord be always with you . . .

1 Corinthians 7.17

17 71.26 *General*

Aim for perfection, listen to my appeal,
be of one mind, live in peace.
Greet one another with a holy kiss.
And the God of love and peace be with you . . .

2 Corinthians 13.11

17 71.27 *General*

Let the peace of Christ rule in your hearts,
since as members of one body you are called to peace.
The peace of the Lord be always with you . . .

Colossians 3.15

72 *WORDS FOR DEDICATION*

These, or other similar responses, may be used at the beginning of the service, at the intercessions, at the Presentation of the Gifts, or before the blessing and dismissal. Gifts of money or tokens of the life and work of the people, or of some particular aspect of service, may be placed on a table in the middle of the congregation or presented to the presiding minister. Some of these responses might also be used for the dedication of church officers and leaders, PCC members, stewardship or mission visitors, etc. This may take place at the intercessions or at the Peace, and the minister may first say, 'As mission visitors (or whatever . . .) we dedicate *ourselves/you* to God's service.'

17 72.1 Christ has offered for all time a single sacrifice for sins.
He is seated at the right hand of God.

Through him let us offer up a sacrifice of praise to God,
the fruit of lips that acknowledge his name.

Do not forget to do good and share what you have.
Such sacrifices are pleasing to God.

17 72.2 The gift of God is eternal life in Christ Jesus our Lord.
By his mercy we present our whole lives to God as a living sacrifice.

17 72.3 Lord Jesus Christ, you emptied yourself,
taking the form of a servant.
Through your love, make us servants of one another.

Lord Jesus Christ, for our sake you became poor.
May our lives and gifts enrich the life of your world.

17 72.4 The free gift of God is eternal life in Christ Jesus our Lord.
By his mercy we present our whole lives to God as a living sacrifice.

Though many, we form one body in Christ.
We belong to one another.

By God's grace we have different gifts.
We will use them in faith.

Rejoice in hope, stand firm in trouble, be constant
in prayer.
Filled with his Spirit we will serve the Lord.

See also *17* 63.12

73 *WORDS AT THE BREAKING OF BREAD*

1 73.1 *Advent*

God of promise,
you prepare a banquet for us in your kingdom.
Happy are those who are called
to the supper of the Lamb!

2 73.2 *Incarnation*

'I am the bread which has come down from heaven', says the Lord.
Give us this bread for ever. *John 6.33,34*

3 73.3 *Epiphany, Light*

We break the bread of life
and that life is the light of the world:
God here among us,
light in the midst of us,
bring us to light and life. *Song of Solomon 4*

4 73.4 *Lent and Holy Week*

Every time we eat this bread
and drink this cup:
we proclaim the Lord's death
until he comes. *1 Corinthians 11.26*

6 73.5 *Resurrection, Heaven, Glory, Transfiguration, Death, Funerals*

Lord, we died with you on the cross.
Now we are raised to new life.

We were buried in your tomb.
Now we share in your resurrection.

Live in us, that we may live in you. *Romans 6.3,4*

9 73.6 *Creation, Harvest, Bread, Vine*

Creator of all,
we have gathered many grains
and made them into this one bread.
We look for your Church to be gathered
from the ends of the earth
into the kingdom. *Didache*

17 73.7 *General*

'I am the bread of life', says the Lord.
'Whoever comes to me will never be hungry;
whoever believes in me will never thirst.'
Taste and see that the Lord is good:
happy are they who trust in him.

John 6.48,51; Psalm 34.8

8 EUCHARISTIC PRAYERS

ALTERNATIVE EUCHARISTIC PRAYER A

The president takes the bread and cup.

We celebrate together the gifts and the grace of God.
We take this bread,
We take this wine,
to follow his example,
and obey his command.

The Lord is here.
His Spirit is with us.

or

The Lord be with you
and also with you.

Lift up your hearts.
We lift them to the Lord.

Let us give thanks to the Lord our God.
It is right to give him thanks and praise.

Blessed are you, Lord, God of the universe,
you bring forth bread from the earth.
Blessed be God for ever.
Blessed are you, Lord, God of the universe,
you create the fruit of the vine.
Blessed be God for ever.
The created universe praise you, its creator.
Sun and rain, hills and rivers praise you.
Blessed be God for ever.
The fruit of the earth itself praises you:
Wheat and grape,this bread and wine we have,
are part of the riches of your earth.
You are worthy, our Lord and God,
to receive glory and honour and power,
for you created all things,
and through your will they have their being.

You made us in your image,
and went on loving us even when we turned against you.
You loved us so much you gave up your Son
that we may no longer be slaves to sin
but rise to life with him.

(*A proper preface may be inserted here*)

You lift us up to join the songs of heaven:
Worthy is the Lamb, the Lamb that was slain,
to receive all power and wealth, wisdom and might,
honour and glory and praise!

Until the kingdom of God comes
we keep the feast that he began.
The night before he died, at supper with his friends
He took bread and gave you thanks.
he broke it and shared it:
'my body, given for you'.

After supper he took the cup of wine:
'The new covenant, sealed with my blood.
Do this in remembrance of me.'
We celebrate his offering of himself
once for all on the cross,
his resurrection, ascension and coming again:

You chose us to be your people
You called us a royal priesthood
We offer you the sacrifice of praise.

or

Dying you destroyed our death
Rising you restored our life
Lord Jesus, come in glory.

We are your new creation in Christ:
Fill us with your Spirit,
to bring good news to the poor,
to heal the broken-hearted,
to announce release to captives
and freedom to prisoners.
As we eat this bread and drink this wine:
Come, Holy Spirit, flow through us,
fill our sacrifice of praise and thanksgiving
with your power and love.

With all in heaven we worship you
in songs of everlasting praise:

Holy, holy, holy Lord,
God of power and might,
heaven and earth are full of your glory.
Hosanna in the highest.

Silence should be kept.

The Lord's Prayer is said either as follows or in its traditional form

As our Saviour taught us, so we pray
Our Father in heaven,
hallowed be your name,

your kingdom come,
your will be done,
on earth as in heaven.
Give us today our daily bread.
Forgive us our sins
as we forgive those who sin against us.
Lead us not into temptation
but deliver us from evil.

For the kingdom, the power, and the glory
are yours
now and for ever. Amen.

The president breaks the consecrated bread, saying

We are one with Christ in praise and glory,
heirs together of his kingdom.
We break this bread to share in his body.
We take and eat to *proclaim* his death today.
We live by faith in the promises of his covenant.
We have this wine to share in his blood.
We take and drink to *proclaim* his death today.

The president and people receive the communion

PROPER PREFACES

Advent
So we look forward to the day when
you will make all things new
as he comes to judge the world.

Incarnation
You shared our life in human form
from the warmth of Mary's womb
to the stillness of the grave.

Epiphany
You have brought us from darkness to light
and made your light shine in our hearts.
You bring us to know your glory
in the face of Jesus Christ.

Cross
Our sins lifted him high on the cross.
He draws the whole world to himself
and we worship him as now. . .

or
He is the true passover lamb
offered for us,
to take away the sin of the world.

Resurrection
By his death he has destroyed death,
and by his rising again
he has restored to us eternal life.
or
By his victory over the grave
he burst the gates of death for ever.

Ascension
He humbled himself to die on a cross
but you raised him high
and gave him the name
above all other names
Jesus Christ our Lord.

Pentecost
Through him we receive the Spirit of adoption,
telling us we are your children,
and crying 'Abba, Father.'

ALTERNATIVE EUCHARISTIC PRAYER B

The Lord is here. *or* The Lord be with you
His Spirit is with us. and also with you.

Lift up your hearts.
We lift them to the Lord.

Let us give thanks to the Lord our God.
It is right to give him thanks and praise.

Blessed are you, Lord God, our light and our salvation;
to you be glory and praise for ever!
From the beginning you have created all things
and all your works echo the silent music of your praise.
In the fullness of time you made us in your image,
the crown of all creation.
You give us breath and speech that with all the powers of heaven
we may find a voice to sing your praise:

Holy, holy, holy Lord,
God of power and might,
heaven and earth are full of your glory.
Hosanna in the highest.

This anthem may also be used
Blessed is he who comes in the name of the Lord.
Hosanna in the highest.

How wonderful the work of your hands, O Lord!
As a mother tenderly gathers her children
you embraced a people as your own. . .★

Insertions (a) optional here (see following pages)

From them you raised up Jesus, our Saviour, born of Mary,
to be the living bread, in whom all our hungers are satisfied . . .★

Insertions (b) optional here (see following pages)

On the night before he suffered on the cross, he came to table
with his friends, he took bread, saying,
'Take this, all of you, and eat.
This is my body which will be given up for you.' ★
After supper, he took the cup, and giving thanks, he said:
'Take this, all of you, and drink my blood of the new covenant,
shed for you and for all, that sins may be forgiven.' ★

Christ has died:
Christ is risen:
Christ will come again.

★ **to you be glory and praise for ever!** may be repeated as an acclamation after each of the asterisked lines.

Father, as we plead with confidence his sacrifice made once for all,
we remember his dying and rising in glory,
and we rejoice that he prays for us at your right hand:
Pour out your Holy Spirit over us and these gifts
which we bring before you from your own creation;
Show them to be for us the body and blood of your dear Son . . . ★

Insertions (c) optional here (see below and following pages)

Through him, with him, and in him,
with all who stand before you in earth and heaven,
we worship you, Father almighty,
in songs of everlasting praise:

Blessing and honour and glory and power
be yours for ever and ever. Amen.

OPTIONAL 'PROPER' INSERTIONS

(a) between lines 11 and 12
(b) between lines 13 and 14
(c) between lines 26 and 27

1 *Ferial*

(a) You filled them with longing for a peace without fear,
a justice that would never fail.

(b) He offered his life for sinners,
and with a love stronger than death
he opened wide his arms on the cross.

(c) May we who eat and drink in his presence
be constant in prayer and strong in love
until all creation is one in Christ.

2 *Bread of Life*

(a) You fed them with manna in the wilderness
as they walked the pilgrim path in your sight.

(b) He broke bread with those whom others scorned
and when the multitude were hungry he fed them
abundantly.

(c) Make us one body, a holy and living sacrifice,
to serve you acceptably as a royal priesthood.

★ **to you be glory and praise for ever!** may be repeated as an acclamation after each of the asterisked lines.

3 *The Vine*

(a) You planted them as your own choice vine,
but again and again they turned from you in sin.

(b) He is the true vine, your chosen one,
in whom we are joined to bear fruit in plenty.

(c) As we taste and see that the Lord is gracious,
may we dwell in him, as he lives in us.

4 *The Spirit*

(a) You promised to pour upon them your Holy Spirit,
that the young might see visions
and the old have dreams of your coming Kingdom.

(b) He breathed upon his disciples the power of your Spirit
to proclaim the good news to all peoples.

(c) Renew the life of your Spirit
in all who share this eucharistic feast.

5 *The Cross*

(a) When they turned away and rebelled
your love remained steadfast.

(b) For our sins he was lifted up
that he might draw the whole world to himself.

(c) Unite in his cross
all who share the food and drink
of his new unending life.

6 *The Saints*

(a) For all your creatures praise you
and your faithful servants bless you.

(b) In him you have received us as your sons and daughters
and made us citizens of your Kingdom.

(c) Gather us into communion with (*N* and) all your saints;
nourish and strengthen us in the life of heaven,
and confirm us in their faith and truth.

7 *The Kingdom*

(a) You spoke to them through prophets
who looked for the day of deliverance to draw near.

(b) He came among us as a servant,
to be Emmanuel, your presence with us.

(c) Gather your Church from the ends of the earth
into your kingdom,
that we, with all your people,
may share the eternal banquet you have promised.

8 *Baptism*

(a) You called them in covenant
to be a light to all the nations.

(b) Through him we are saved for ever
and baptized into your service.

(c) By the baptism of water and your Holy Spirit
may we witness to your truth in all the world
until he comes in final victory.

and/or
Remember your Church in every land,
redeemed by the blood of your Christ.
Reveal her unity, guard her faith,
and preserve her in peace.
Remember all who minister in your Church. . .
Remember those baptized this day. . .

9 *Penitence*

(a) Again and again you forgave them
and restored them to your love.

(b) By his death he broke the power of sin
and made us holy through his blood.

(c) At this table make us one in Christ,
open to us a new and living way into your presence.

10 *Incarnation*

(a) You taught them to hope for salvation,
the joy of every longing heart.

(b) He was born in the poverty of a stable,
to make known the riches of your kingdom.

(c) As we break this bread and share this cup,
may we know the presence of your Word made flesh.

11 *Resurrection*

(a) You delivered them from slavery
and brought them to the promised land.

(b) By his victory over the grave
he burst the gates of death for ever.

(c) Shine through the darkness of our doubt and sorrow
that the light of his risen presence
may brighten the path before us.

12 *City*

(a) You gave them the hope of a city
the place of unity and peace.

(b) He gave up his life outside the city gate
and opened for all the way to heaven.

(c) Dwell among us as we journey to the new Jerusalem
to be your people, where our God reigns for ever.

ALTERNATIVE EUCHARISTIC PRAYER C

The Lord is here. *or* The Lord be with you
His Spirit is with us. **and also with you.**

Lift up your hearts.
We lift them to the Lord.

Let us give thanks to the Lord our God.
It is right to give him thanks and praise.

Lord God of justice and mercy,
you care for the world and for each of us;
we glorify your name.
You call us to share your life and you give us your love.
You are a kind and compassionate Father,
always ready to forgive.
You rejoice in our joy, listen patiently to our troubles,
and comfort us in distress.

Father we glorify your name for ever.

You show your love in Jesus Christ your Word made flesh.
He is your Good News to the world; through him we are saved.
He gave up his life on the cross to gain forgiveness for us.

Risen* Lord, we praise you.

At supper the night before he died, he took bread and broke it,
giving you thanks and praise.
He gave it to his disciples and said:
'This is my body given for you.'

Jesus, you are the living bread.

At the end of supper he took the cup of wine and said:
'This cup is the New Covenant in my blood.
Drink it in remembrance of me.'

Jesus, you are the true vine.

God of all holiness, we are gathered in your name
to celebrate the sacrifice Jesus made for us all.
As we do this in remembrance of him,
May your Spirit show these gifts of bread and wine
to be for us his saving body and blood.

Holy Spirit, you are the Power of God.

Lord and giver of life,
help us to work together for your kingdom,

---

*This may be changed seasonally to 'Ascended', 'Crucified', 'Lord born of Mary', etc.

and for that day when your justice and mercy
will be seen everywhere.
By your grace unite us in Christ with your whole Church
on earth and in heaven,
so that with one voice we may worship you
and praise your name:

Holy, holy, holy is the Lord God Almighty,
who was, and is and is to come.
To him be honour and glory for ever and ever. Amen.

or

Holy, holy, holy Lord,
God of power and might,
heaven and earth are full of your glory.
Hosanna in the highest.

Silence should be kept.

The Lord's Prayer is said either as follows or in its traditional form.

As our Saviour taught us, so we pray.
Our Father in heaven,
hallowed be your name,
your kingdom come,
your will be done,
on earth as in heaven.
give us today our daily bread.
Forgive us our sins
as we forgive those who sin against us.
Lead us not into temptation
but deliver us from evil.

For the kingdom, the power, and the glory
are yours
now and for ever. Amen.

The president breaks the consecrated bread, either in silence or saying this or another authorized form.

We break this bread
to share in the body of Christ.
Though we are many, we are one body,
because we all share in one bread.

(then Rite A sections 44-46)

ALTERNATIVE EUCHARISTIC PRAYER D

The Lord is here. *or* The Lord be with you
His Spirit is with us. **and also with you.**

Lift up your hearts.
We lift them to the Lord.

Let us give thanks to the Lord our God.
It is right to give him thanks and praise.

For the Preface, one of the Thanksgivings from the Praise section of this book must be used. It may begin with

Father, we give you thanks and praise
through Jesus Christ your Son, our Lord,
because . . .

and end

So, with angels and archangels, and all the company of heaven,
we praise you for ever, saying

Holy, holy, holy Lord,
God of power and might,
heaven and earth are full of your glory.
Hosanna in the highest.

This anthem may also be used
Blessed is he who comes in the name of the Lord.
Hosanna in the highest.

Praise and thanks to you, Father in heaven:
on the night before he died
your Son Jesus Christ took bread and wine.
He gave thanks and said
This is my body, given for you.
This is my blood, shed for the forgiveness of sins.

Christ has died:
Christ is risen:
Christ will come again.

Pour out your Holy Spirit
as we bring before you these gifts
and remember his sacrifice
made once for all on the cross.
Feed us with his body and blood,
that we may live and grow in him.

Through him we worship you, Father almighty,
in songs of everlasting praise:

**Blessing and honour and glory and power
be yours for ever and ever. Amen.**

Silence should be kept.

The Lord's Prayer is said either as follows or in its traditional form.

As our Saviour taught us, so we pray.
**Our Father in heaven,
hallowed be your name,
your kingdom come,
your will be done,
on earth as in heaven.
Give us today our daily bread.
Forgive us our sins
as we forgive those who sin against us.
Lead us not into temptation
but deliver us from evil.**

**For the kingdom, the power, and the glory
are yours
now and for ever. Amen.**

The president breaks the consecrated bread, either in silence or saying this or another authorized form.

We break this bread
to share in the body of Christ.
**Though we are many, we are one body,
because we all share in one bread.**

(then Rite A sections 44-46)

ALTERNATIVE FORMS OF 'HOLY, HOLY'
ALTERNATIVE ACCLAMATIONS

1 HOLY, HOLY

Part or all of a song which is a version of 'Holy, holy', such as the following, may replace the 'Holy, Holy'

Holy, holy, holy is the Lord;
Holy is the Lord God almighty!
Holy, holy, holy is the Lord;
Holy is the Lord God almighty!
Who was, and is, and is to come;
Holy, holy, holy is the Lord!

Jesus, Jesus, Jesus is the Lord;
Jesus is the Lord God almighty!
Jesus, Jesus, Jesus is the Lord;
Jesus is the Lord God almighty!
Who was, and is, and is to come;
Holy, holy, holy is the Lord!

Worthy, worthy, worthy is the Lord;
Worthy is the Lord God almighty!
Worthy, worthy, worthy is the Lord;
Worthy is the Lord God almighty!
Who was, and is, and is to come;
Holy, holy, holy is the Lord!

Glory, glory, glory to the Lord;
Glory to the Lord God almighty!
Glory, glory, glory to the Lord;
Glory to the Lord God almighty!
Who was, and is, and is to come;
Holy, holy, holy is the Lord!

2 ACCLAMATIONS

These may be used with any of the Eucharistic Prayers in Rite A, or with those above.

1 **Dying you destroyed our death,**
rising you restored our life.
Lord Jesus, come in glory.

2 **When we eat this bread and drink this cup,**
we proclaim your death, Lord Jesus,
until you come in glory.

3 **Lord, by your cross and resurrection**
you have set us free.
You are the Saviour of the world.

4 **You chose us to be your people.**
You called us a royal priesthood.
We offer you our sacrifice of praise.

5 **With this bread and this cup**
we show forth Christ's death
until he comes in glory.

9 BLESSINGS AND ENDINGS

Section 54 in Rite A Holy Communion permits the president to say an alternative blessing. Some are provided in section 77 of the service, and two more as sections 18 and 19 in Prayers for Various Occasions. The ASB structure is easy to copy, to provide a blessing to fit with a special occasion or some particular emphasis in the worship or teaching: an opening sentence which is a prayer that God will do something, followed by that form of the blessing popularized by medieval bishops:

'. . . and the blessing of God almighty,
the Father, the Son, and the Holy Spirit,
be among you and remain with you always.'

Some further examples of that form are provided here, together with some alternative structures, one of which is the three-part solemn blessing. This focuses on some biblical story or doctrine, relates that to what we believe, and prays for a deepening of our experience of that aspect of God's work, summed up in the same form of blessing.

The dismissal, ending or blessing should always be the last item in any service, and should not be followed by a hymn or more prayers.

1 9.1 *Advent*

God sent his Son our Saviour Jesus Christ
to come among us in great humility.
You look for him to come again in power and
great glory:
Amen.
You rejoice at our Redeemer's birth to live with us.
As you live in the light of his coming,
may he free you from sin and make you holy,
steadfast in faith, constant in love and joyful in hope:
Amen.
And when he comes again in glory
may he reward you with endless life:
Amen.
And the blessing . . .

1 9.2 *Advent*

Christ the Son of righteousness shine upon you and
make you ready to meet him when he comes in glory;
and the blessing . . .

1 9.3 *Advent*

May God himself, the God of peace,
make you perfect and holy;
and keep you all safe and blameless, in spirit, soul
and body,
for the coming of our Lord Jesus Christ:
and the blessing . . .

1 Thessalonians 5.23

2 9.4 *Incarnation, Christmas, Annunciation, Mary*

God sent his angels from glory to bring to shepherds
the good news of our Saviour's birth:
Amen.
You have seen his glory,
the glory of the Father's only Son:
Amen.
May he fill you with joy
and send you out from his glory
to bring this good news to others today:
Amen.
And the blessing . . .

2 9.5 *Incarnation, Christmas*

Jesus Christ was born of the Virgin Mary:
revealed in his glory;

worshipped by angels:
proclaimed among the nations;

exalted to the highest heavens:
believed in throughout the world.

Blessed be God, our strength and our salvation:
now and for ever. Amen.

2 9.6 *Mothering Sunday, Mary*

When the Word became flesh
earth was joined to heaven in the womb of Mary:
may the love and obedience of Mary be your example.
Amen.

May the peace of Christ
rule in your hearts and homes.
Amen.

May you be filled with the joys of the Spirit
and the gifts of your eternal home.
Amen.
And the blessing . . .

3 9.7 *Epiphany, Light*

God led the wise men by the shining of a star
to find Christ, the light from light.
May he lead you also in your pilgrimage,
to meet your Lord:
Amen.
You believe God has brought you out of darkness
to share with his saints in the kingdom of light,
the kingdom of his Son:
Amen.
May the light of his glorious gospel shine in your hearts,
transform your lives,
and bring his light to others:
Amen.
And the blessing . . .

Colossians 1.13; 1 Corinthians 4.4

3 9.8 *Epiphany, Light*

May Christ draw you to humility and worship,
and bring you to see God at work;
and the blessing. . .

3 9.9 *Epiphany, Wedding*

God sent his Son
to provide new wine of joy
at a wedding in Cana:
Amen.
You believe God cares for us
and still has the power that turned water into wine.
May you experience the kindness and blessings
of his presence:
Amen.
May he work miracles in your lives, make glad your hearts, and change you day by day to reflect his glory, until that day when you see him face to face:
Amen.
And the blessing. . .

John 2.1-11

4 9.10 *Lent, Penitence*

You believe God will not despise
a broken spirit and a contrite heart:
Amen.
You believe Christ bore your sins
in his body on the tree;
you have been healed by his wounds:
Amen.
May he give you a spirit of repentance day by day,
pardon, peace, and the assurance of sins forgiven:
Amen.
And the blessing. . . *Psalm 51;Isaiah 53*

5 9.11 *Cross*

You believe that by his dying
Christ destroyed death for ever:
Amen.
You have been crucified with Christ
and live by faith in the Son of God,
who loved you and gave himself for you:
Amen.
May he send you out to glory in his cross,
and live no longer for yourselves but for him,
who died and was raised to life for us:
Amen.
And the blessing. . . *Galatians 2.20, 2 Corinthians 5.15*

6 9.12 *Transfiguration*

God of our forebears, who called you to reflect his eternal glory in Christ Jesus, transform you by his Spirit to an ever greater degree of glory;
and the blessing. . .

6 9.13 *Resurrection, Heaven, Glory, Transfiguration, Death, Funerals*

You believe Jesus has been raised from the dead
in glory:
Amen.
You believe you have been raised with Christ:
Amen.
May your hearts and minds be set on things above,
where Christ is seated at the right hand of God;
and the blessing. . . *Colossians 3.1,2*

6 9.14 *Resurrection, Heaven, Glory, Transfiguration, Death, Funerals*

May Christ, who out of defeat
brings new hope and a new future,
fill you with his new life;
and the blessing. . .

6 9.15 *Heaven*

God and Father of our Lord Jesus Christ,
bring us to the dwelling which your Son
is preparing for all who love you.
Amen.
Give us the will each day
to live in life eternal.
Amen.
Let our citizenship be in heaven
with your blessed and beloved,
the whole company of the redeemed.
Amen.
And the blessing of God almighty,
the Father, the Son, and the Holy Spirit,
be upon us and remain with us always.
Amen.

7 9.16 *Ascension, Kingship*

Christ our exalted King
pour upon you his abundant gifts
and bring you to reign with him in glory;
and the blessing. . .

7 9.17 *Ascension, Kingship*

You believe Jesus has ascended to heaven
to prepare a place for you:
Amen.
You believe Jesus has taken his seat in majesty
at the right hand of the Father:
Amen.
May you have the joy of experiencing
that he is with you to the end of time
according to his promise;
Amen.
And the blessing. . . *Matthew 28.16-20*

7 9.18 *Ascension, Kingship*

Yours, Lord, is the greatness, the power,
the glory, the splendour, and the majesty:
for everything in heaven and on earth is yours.
Yours, Lord, is the kingdom:
and you are exalted as head over all. Amen.
1 Chronicles 29.11

8 9.19 *Spirit, Pentecost, Gifts, Healing, Baptism and Confirmation*

You believe God poured out his promised Holy Spirit
on the day of Pentecost:
Amen.
You believe you have been baptized with the Spirit
and with fire:
Amen.
May his tongues of flame
burn out all evil from your hearts,
fill you with his love and peace,
and give you the gifts of his Spirit
and a voice to praise him for ever,
Amen.
And the blessing. . . *Acts 2.1-4*

8 9.20 *Spirit, Pentecost, Gifts, Healing, Baptism and Confirmation*

May Christ's holy, healing, enabling Spirit be with you
and guide you on your way at every change and turn;
and the blessing. . .

8 9.21 *Spirit, Pentecost, Gifts, Healing, Baptism and Confirmation*

May the God of hope fill us
with all joy and peace in believing,
through the power of the Holy Spirit.
Amen. *Romans 15.13*

8 9.22 *Trinity*

The Lord bless you and keep you:
Amen.
The Lord make his face to shine upon you,
and be gracious to you:
Amen.

The Lord lift up his countenance upon you
and give you peace:
Amen.
The Lord God almighty, Father, Son, and Holy Spirit,
the holy and undivided Trinity,
guard you, save you,
and bring you to that heavenly city,
where he lives and reigns for ever and ever:
Amen. *Numbers 6.24-25*

10 9.23 *Word*

Hear the teaching of Jesus:
'Blessed are those who hear the word of God
and obey it.'
Go now to do God's will,
and the blessing. . .

10 9.24 *Word*

Go now in peace,
knowing that you have been born again,
not of perishable seed,
but of imperishable,
through the living and enduring word of God,
and the blessing. . .

11 9.25 *Church, Mission and Ministry, Unity*

Glory to God:
whose power, working in us,
can do infinitely more
than we ask or imagine.
Glory to God from generation to generation,
in the Church and in Christ Jesus,
for ever and ever. Amen. *Ephesians 3.20-21*

11 9.26 *Church, Mission and Ministry, Unity*

May God who gives patience and encouragement
give you a spirit of unity
to live in harmony as you follow Jesus Christ,
so that with one voice you may glorify
the God and Father of our Lord Jesus Christ.
Amen.

Romans 15.5,6

12 9.27 *City, World and Society*

God, who has prepared for you
a city with permanent foundations,
bring you to the eternal and triumphant joy
of that city of the great King;
and the blessing. . .

13 9.28 *Family*

May the Father from whom every family
in earth and heaven receives its name
strengthen you with his Spirit in your inner being,
so that Christ may dwell in your hearts by faith,
and that, knowing his love,
broad and long, deep and high beyond
our knowledge,
you may be filled with all the fullness of God;
and the blessing. . .

Ephesians 3.15-19

14 9.29 *Saints*

God has given you, in the lives of his saints,
patterns of holy living and victorious dying.
He has made it possible for you to join with his saints,
and with them to inherit the light:
Amen.
May the God and Father of our Lord Jesus Christ
give you the spirit of wisdom and revelation
to know the hope to which he has called you,
the riches of the glorious inheritance
promised to his saints:
Amen.
You are no longer strangers and aliens,
but live as fellow-citizens of all the saints
in God's house.
May you set your hearts and minds on things above,
where Christ is seated at the right hand of God:
Amen.
And the blessing. . .

Colossians 1.12; Ephesians 1.17,18; 2.14

14 9.30 *Saints*

May Christ who makes saints of sinners,
who has transformed those we remember today,

raise and strengthen you that you may transform
the world;
and the blessing. . .

15 9.31 *Kingdom, Freedom, Reconciliation*

Now may the blessing of God the Father,
who made from one every nation
that occupies the earth;
of God the Son, who bought us for God
from every tribe and language
and people and nation;
and of God the Spirit, who brings us together in unity,
be with us and remain with us always.
Amen. *Acts 17.26; Revelation 5.9*

15 9.32 *Kingdom, Advent*

May God the Father, judge all merciful,
make us worthy of a place in his kingdom:
Amen.
May God the Son, coming among us in power,
reveal among us the promise of his glory:
Amen.
May God the Holy Spirit make us steadfast in faith,
joyful in hope and constant in love:
Amen.
And the blessing of God almighty,
the Father, the Son and the Holy Spirit,
be upon you and remain with always.
Amen.

16 9.33 *Love, Marriage*

May God the Father join you together
in mutual love and faithful living,
as he united Adam and Eve, our first parents:
Amen.
May the Lord Jesus be present with you,
to bless your marriage with all his power
and gladden your hearts with the joy of Cana:
Amen.
May the Holy Spirit fill you with a life of strength
and patience,
and crown you with the blessing of his heavenly gifts:
Amen.
And the blessing. . .

17 9.34 *General*

The Lord God almighty is our Father:
He loves us and cares tenderly for us.
The Lord Jesus Christ is our Saviour:
He has redeemed us and will defend us to the end.
The Lord, the Holy Spirit, is among us:
He will lead us in God's holy way.
To God almighty, Father, Son and Holy Spirit,
be praise and glory today and for ever. Amen.

17 9.35 *General*

The almighty and merciful Lord, Father, Son, and
Holy Spirit, bless us and keep us. **Amen.**

17 9.36 *General*

Now may the Lord of peace himself
give you peace at all times and in every way.
The Lord be with you all;
and the blessing. . . *2 Thessalonians 3.16*

17 9.37 *General*

You are called and loved by God the Father
and kept safe by Jesus Christ:
Mercy, peace and love be yours in abundance,
from God the Father, Son and Holy Spirit.
Amen. *Jude 1,2*

17 9.38 *General*

May God give to you and to all those you love
his comfort and his peace,
his light and his joy,
in this world and the next,
and the blessing. . .

17 9.39 *General*

Let us bless the Lord:
Thanks be to God.
Blessing, honour and glory be yours,
here and everywhere,
now and for ever. Amen.

THE COMMENTARY
SAMPLE SECTIONS

The pages that follow are placed here so that readers can form a view as to whether this way of providing instruction and discussion material as part of our provision for worship is helpful. The intention is to provide guidance on all the main elements in the service, as well as a few general areas such as preparation, how to combine and insert other services and actions, and how to produce a printed version of a service for local use.

INTRODUCTION

WHY THIS IS HERE AND HOW TO USE IT

Worship is not worship until you do it.

It is no longer sufficient in the Church of England to produce a worship book which consists simply of texts, to say or sing. That is a bit like producing a recipe which is a list of ingredients without the instructions for putting them together.

But how do you offer advice and suggest questions to ask about the presentation of the liturgy without putting it all in rubrics, or mandatory stage-instructions, in the services, or producing a separate manual? We decided the most digestible and least legalistic way of doing it would be to tell stories. So here you have the stories of four entirely imaginary churches, told in sections which correspond with the Resource Sections. As you read them, you will gather a little of the flavour and style of each church, town and country, with different spaces and resources. You may find you identify more with one than with another, but be prepared to learn from the others.

How to use it

It is not necessary to read right through the commentary. Those wishing to look at the presentation of a particular area of worship might get two or three people to read that particular section of the commentary. It might help to offer them some questions to ask:

> Can you imagine being present in the situations described?
>
> What is good or bad about them?
>
> Do you feel nearer to the experience of one of the four churches?

Which one?

Make a list of suggestions which come to you as a result of reading this section.

Are any of these suggestions possible for us

(a) some time in the future?

(b) right now?

Do we need variety in how we handle this week by week, or do we need the security of being consistent?

Do we need to consult with others before taking action – other church leaders, the PCC, musicians, choir, servers, etc.?

What is worship?

A worship planning group, a PCC or church leaders' group would do well to have some discussion in general terms about worship. Are we agreed about what is worship and what is not, what the ingredients are, what kind of movement, physical, emotional and spiritual, we should expect in worship?

Try completing the sentence, 'Worship is . . .'. Yes, it is giving God his worth, or what he deserves, or glory. 'The true end of man is to glorify God and enjoy him for ever', as they said in the seventeenth century. But explore the mechanics of that a bit more: do any of these sentences get near our experience?

Worship is a door open in heaven. We lift up our hearts, listen in to what God is saying, join the angels and archangels and all the saints in heaven in praising God's eternal holiness. We are there and he is here.

Worship is a door open to the inner depths of life. Suddenly, as we worship, there is wholeness, *shalom*, peace, as all the fragmented bits of our being are put into God's perspective. Things make sense, and there is something to hold on to which has hitherto seemed just beyond the grasp of our mind.

Worship is a door open to the rhythms of life. Through festivals, simple rituals, a weekly rhythm, worship marking morning and evening, the whole of life, time and space is claimed for God and given back to him. In the worship he gives it to us again, to use for him, and we know he is concerned with our hopes and fears, politics and problems, families and finance.

Worship is a door to our hearts open in obedience to God. He commands us to worship in spirit and in truth. We respond to the overwhelming majesty of his beauty revealed in creation, to his overwhelming love and grace revealed in his word and in his Son. And as we worship, we are changed . . .

Now, this is in no sense an agreed definition of worship. Rather, it is intended to stimulate local parish groups and worship leaders to arrive at some agreement on what they expect, or are longing for, in their worship.

PRELIMINARY FACTORS

A Imagination, vision and patterns

St Ann's is a large urban/suburban church, with a mixed congregation of different ages and backgrounds. There is considerable lay involvement in the leadership of the church, and this is evident in the worship too. The PCC recently spent a day away reviewing the church's worship, and one of the results of this was the setting up of a Worship Group (see opposite page and *Planning and Preparation,* below).

Sunday worship is the centrepoint and focus of the whole life of this very active church, and a lot of energy is put into preparing for Sunday both by those involved in teaching the different adult and children's groups and by the music and drama groups. Sunday morning worship is on the Rite A Holy Communion pattern every week, but making use of the provisions in *Patterns for Worship* for the first half to have the flavour of a family service. There are, regularly, adult groups, video and other ways of doing the sermon, and a break at the Peace when the children come back from their groups and some non-communicants and enquirers can leave without embarrassment.

St Ann's day away agenda

1 Prayer

2 Share in twos or threes what is really good about our worship.

3 Talk or Bible study or discussion:

'What is worship?'

'What should our Sunday worship include?'

4 From this, in twos and threes, list two or three principles which should govern our worship. Share these with the whole group, and see how much agreement there is. Sometimes we disagree on practical decisions about worship because we don't agree on the principles.

5 Next, consider in small groups practical questions such as:

How does the worship meet the needs of the elderly, children of different ages, the disabled, those who find reading difficult, those who need to be stretched intellectually? How should we expect to know the presence of God? How could the intercessions be improved? Should there be more freedom (or less?) in our worship?

Then decide which two items should come top of the group's agenda.

6 With everyone together, list the suggested agenda items, see how much overlap there is, and start with the one with most 'votes'. There will not be time to discuss everything. Some items will need further research: two people could be briefed to bring items back to the PCC.

7 For each item, consider four questions.

What resources do we need?

What barriers or problems are there in the way of taking action on this?

What is the timetable for action?

Who is responsible for action?

St Christopher's programme for Sunday evenings

6.00 1662 Evening prayer

6.45 A simple devotional or sacramental meditation

7.00 Coffee

7.15 Singing and worship

Most prople stay all the time, though some come just for the first hour or the second hour. Both the meditation and the informal singing and worship time are used for introducing new songs and material such as that in *Patterns*.

St Bartholomew's is a lovely mediaeval country church, small both in size and in congregation. Sharing a vicar with other churches in the group means that the Sunday pattern varies from week to week, and the main service is not always communion. The church is not as insular as it used to be, with one or two people sometimes going to services at other churches in the group, and some 'new' people in the village bringing experience of other churches. The main vision of the staff (vicar, deacon and an excellent reader), is for worship that is accessible to everyone in the village, children included, and accurately reflects and sums up the life of the community. Some of the congregation would prefer it to be a little less related to the community, and more of a beautiful oasis, away from the week's troubles, a kind of entering into eternity from which they can emerge refreshed to face the week.

St Christopher's is a large nineteenth-century mock-gothic building in the downtown part of the city. The parish priest lives in the vicarage adjoining the church – the high brick wall also includes the disused school now used adventurously for a wide range of community activities – and he is the only professional living in the area. The small congregation spend a lot of time together: all of them live locally. Some of them help to run things in the community centre and every morning there are four or five praying, with more for late evening worship, and thirty for communion with hymns and sermon on Tuesday evening. Sunday worship is a culmination and gathering together of the activities, concerns and worship of the week. The social needs of the community are offered to God as easily as they are discussed practically in the pub after church – a kind of extended Peace attended by most of the congregation.

St David's is a church where worship is simply not one of the most important things the church does. It comes low on most people's agenda, though there are occasional heated discussions at the PCC. The demands of different factions and rival views in the church mean that the worship is very bitty, and there is a different kind of service each Sunday in the month, with very few people going every week. The vicar finds little time for preparation and feels he cannot involve others in preparing or helping to lead because of the need to keep the balance between the different factions.

B Architecture, space and colour

St Ann's is a modern building with worshippers seated on moveable chairs in a semi-circle around the shallow open dais. The amplification system is excellent and none of the furniture in the building is fixed. A creative group in the church makes banners and throw-away paper visuals which focus on the season or the teaching theme – and the children's groups often contribute their own decorations. Using free-standing screens for some of these means that they need not always be in the same place, and can be moved according to the needs of the worship. It also avoids sticky messes on the walls, though occasionally the wall is used, as when they went for a year or so with the words 'Christ has died, Christ is risen, Christ will come again' in lovely paper letters on the wall behind the holy table.

St Bartholomew's found some years ago that they could increase the sense of space in their tiny church by removing the back row of the choir, moving the front stalls back, and putting carpet right across the chancel and sanctuary. At the same time, they moved the altar forward far enough for the president to get behind it.

More recently, they have looked at the need for somewhere for a very small group to worship on Sunday evenings or for less formal midweek occasions. The result of this has been the transformation of a small side chapel. The floor has been levelled (a sanctuary step had been put in at some stage), an efficient independent heating system installed, the old wooden chairs replaced by stacking cushioned stools, whose upholstery matches the carpet and the new pastel wash on the walls. And the small Jacobean table, restored and no longer boxed in with hangings, is a fitting focus for the seven or eight who gather round. Other 'focus' items include an icon of the Trinity and a single candle. Worshipping in this situation, with more personal relationship between the members of the congregation and the president, inevitably has an effect on what happens in the larger group on Sundays, and has been a suitable place for trying some of the less formal structures in *Patterns for Worship*.

St Christopher's have only been back in church for a month. They worshipped in the school hall while the church was being re-ordered and decorated, and found this a surprisingly valuable experience. They took a deliberate decision not to cart bits of furniture out of the church into the hall to make the place 'more like church' – they had seen the odd effect of this in another local church which used a community centre, with plastic chairs (each

St Ann's checklist

At their monthly worship planning meeting, the St Ann's leaders check through a number of items to do with space, colour and the use of the building:

1 Should the seating be in the normal arrangement or do we need to change it – make the aisles wider for a procession or dancing, for instance?

2 Are we making the best use of the different spaces? Could we, for example, do a dramatic reading from different parts of the building?

3 Can we visualise the different colours in use on any one day, in the dress of the ministers, banners and other hangings or visuals? Are there times when we might need to use the coloured stage lights?

4 Plot the movement of people in each service, decide if there are clear 'ceremonial routes' for the ministers e.g. moving to the font for a baptism with a family coming forward. Who is responsible for taking care of mechanical hiccups like moving an overhead projector or microphone stand out of the way?

5 What does the church smell and look like? Do we need polish, air freshener or incense?

Small groups

Small groups at worship include not only small Sunday congregations, but those who gather midweek, church leaders and others praying daily, and one minister at prayer on his or her own. *St Bartholomew's* discussed the importance of:

1 The scale of the worship area. A small group is de-scaled by a large and lofty building and made to feel insignificant.

2 Warmth and comfort. It is easier to worship when people are comfortable.

3 Colour. Gentle colours are better for a group close to them, more strident colours for distant and dramatic viewing.

4 Flexible seating. This can be arranged so that people can look at each other or have something as the focus – altar table, icon, candle, banner, lectern or bible.

5 Space, so that movement is possible, not only to come and go with ease, but to move during the worship.

6 The possibility of using the area for one-to-one counselling, ministry to couples, spiritual direction.

How St Christopher's moved

1 Some months of teaching about worship led to most people seeing the present layout could be improved.

2 Vicar and churchwardens met the archdeacon, who outlined possibilities and offered a list of other churches who had made similar changes.

3 PCC set up a small group to visit other churches, get ideas, take measurements and report back.

4 Full-scale on-site consultation between the PCC committee, architect, archdeacon and some members of the Diocesan Advisory Committee and Diocesan Liturgical Committee looked at how proposed changes might help or hinder the worship – bearing in mind the need for flexibility as the exact ways of doing the worship might change.

5 The PCC rightly thought that it was important for people to have a feel of what it would be like before taking the final decision. They considered asking the architect to produce some artist's impressions of what the church would look like, from different points, to be mounted on large display boards. But they decided on an experimental moving of the furniture (by the congregation and therefore at no cost).

6 After a couple of months the PCC consulted every member of the congregation – which made raising the money easier, as everyone felt they had a stake in the decision.

7 Unanimous PCC decision to apply for a faculty, plus careful discussion about how the cost could be cut by doing some of the work themselves.

with its embroidered hassock) and metal tables (one of them with a Victorian frontal not quite fitting it), a heavy gothic lectern and sanctuary chairs to match.

Instead, they decided to use the school furniture as it was, with a white cloth on the table and all the links with church centred on the people and the colourful vestments of the ministers. Without hassocks, they stood for the whole of the Eucharistic Prayer – and quite a bit more in the worship – and decided to carry on doing this when they returned to church. Doing without the organ was a good experience, too, and opened up the possibility of using other instruments regularly. A flute, guitar and piano now practise each week for some of the items in each service, and taped music provides the background to receiving communion more often than the organ.

In the re-ordered St Christopher's, the choir stalls have been moved to the West end of the church, behind the congregation. The chancel, cleared of furniture, is made more spacious with a platform built forward of the chancel arch – with a carpet unifying the floor area. Gone are the heavy oak clergy desks and ornate bishop's chair, replaced by simple seats for the president and his assistants, facing the people. The lectern too is a simple design. The altar has been brought forward, under the arch, with plenty of space for movement round it. There is also space, at the side, for a modern one-piece font, big enough for an adult to stand in and have water poured over him, and incorporating a bowl at waist height for sprinking.

St David's is a bit like an old fashioned museum, with generations of furnishings and clutter which no one is allowed to touch. The sanctuary houses banners from long-departed church organisations, a large three-dimensional marble monument on one wall, a threadbare strip of carpet with brass fasteners, and a holy table which is not a table but a boxed-in wooden framework to hold ancient frontals (and behind which the flower vases, spare candles and watering can are kept). The light oak modern reading desks (given in memory of a benefactor twenty years ago and therefore immoveable – one reason why the table cannot be moved forward) contrast with the dark pine empty choir stalls. And there are some items taken from the now-demolished church in the next parish when it was amalgamated with St David's – an enormous carved oak lectern out of all proportion to the rest of the furnishings, and a large marble font. This was so heavy that a special concrete base had to be built for it at the back of the church (where it is never used). They even found space to cram in a few more pews at the same time, and all without thinking of seeking advice or getting a faculty.

Culture and language

Guidelines on language

These guidelines may help those writing their own material, for intercessions for example, to be on the same level of language as the new writing in *Patterns*.

1 Use concrete visual images rather than language which is conceptual and full of ideas.

2 Avoid complicated sentence constructions.

3 If there is a choice, prefer the word with fewer syllables.

4 Address God as you.

5 Keep sentences as short as possible. Use full stops rather than semicolons.

6 Use language that includes women as well as men.

7 Watch the rhythm. The language should be rhythmic and flow easily, but take care not to have a repetitive poetic 'dum-de-dum'.

8 Liturgical language should not be stark nor empty. It is not wrong to repeat ideas or say the same thing twice in different words. Cranmer recognised that people need time and repetition to make the liturgy their own: we need to do it without a string of dependent clauses.

9 Be prepared to throw it away after using it, and to do it differently next time.

Planning and preparation

At *St Bartholomew's* the vicar recognised the difficulty of planning worship for several different country churches. In St Bartholomew's the monthly Family Service is planned and led by a group of young parents, two of whom teach in the small Sunday School, so that there is some link between the two. They plan the themes six months at a time with the vicar, decide on how to handle the theme in terms of teaching, readings, music, prayers, etc. In one village two people have been on a diocesan course on leading worship, and can plan and lead the first part of the Service of the Word until the vicar arrives. In another village the PCC is small enough to discuss worship easily and the vicar has been training some of them to lead the intercessions.

St Ann's sent three lay leaders on a diocesan course on preparing worship. As a result they came back wanting to set up a planning group for worship. They brought back with them draft terms of reference for such a group, which were discussed amended by the PCC. (See opposite page). The PCC recognised this was a move away from the previous pattern, where a different housegroup had planned and led the worship each week. This had resulted in some inconsistency in the worship, though one good thing about it was that a very wide range of people had been involved, so the new planning group had quite a long list of people in the church who had worship gifts.

Planning at *St Christopher's* is in the hands of the staff. The vicar uses a blank form (specimen opposite) which gradually gets filled in, from his initial ideas a couple of months ahead, through discussion with the staff and regular meetings with Sunday School leaders, organist and head server. Copies of the form, duly typed, give all concerned a complete menu for each service.

The vicar of *St David's* returned from a (compulsory) diocesan clergy conference, at which worship had been on the agenda, keen to put into practice some of the things he had learnt others were doing. Next Sunday's worship was a different structure, with a new confession, creed and Eucharistic Prayer (and no time for the congregation to be taught about them or even to read quietly through them before having to join in). There were also new songs – in the order of service badly duplicated on dark pink paper. The clearest liturgical refrain in the service was 'You'll find it on your pink slip' which amused everyone but the colour-blind. An angry PCC the next week invoked the provisions of the Worship and Doctrine Measure and insisted on a return to the traditional services. Everyone was hurt and the worship was fossilised.

Worship Action Group
Terms of Reference

1. To review and evaluate all aspects of worship at St Ann's, including:

structures and patterns of worship on Sunday;

the relationship between worship and the rest of the life of the church;

the use of music, drama, dance, action, visual elements including robes and ceremonial;

the teaching and preaching programme:

the place of children and other groups.

2. To be responsible for the planning and preparation of Sunday worship, including working through other groups such as house groups, choir, music groups, drama group.

3. To ensure that the varied gifts of the congregation are being used in worship.

4. To plan developments in worship and to prepare for regular PCC discussion of worship.

St Christopher's Service form:
10.30 am Parish Eucharist

Season/mood:
President:
Assistants:
Standard service:
Setting:
Introit/
introductory music/
sentence:
Hymn:
(Old Testament:)
(canticle/song:)
(New Testament:)
Psalm:
Gospel:
Sermon:
Intercessions:
(who? add items . . .)

Any special requirements e.g. tapes, visuals:
Variable items for eucharist (words/music for peace, preface, before and during distribution, postcommunion sentence)

Hymn:
Post-communion prayer:
Notices (list . . .)
Blessing/dismissal:

1 Introductions

Whilst the large and lively mixed-age congregation arrive for worship, the *St Ann's* music group plays a selection of thematic hymns and choruses, in order to focus people's attention on worship, and to set the initial mood of the service.

The congregation join in the singing; the song numbers have been printed on the service sheet. The music stops three or four minutes before the ministers enter and take their places. The congregation becomes quiet, attentive and prayerful – a sense of expectancy is in the air. The minister rises to call the people to worship with a seasonal scripture sentence and congregational response. This is followed by the opening hymn of praise.

At *St Bartholomew's* the organist quietly plays some simple Handel on the small village organ whilst the congregation arrive for worship. The minister has hurried from another village church in the parish, and makes his way to the vestry in order to robe and to have a few moments of prayer before the service begins. The sacristan has taken care to ensure that everything is prepared for worship before the minister arrives. The opening hymn is announced by the minister from the back of the church. As the congregation sing, he makes his way to his place. At the end of the hymn, he greets the congregation with a seasonal sentence, and invites them to join with him in some moments of silence before saying a prayer of preparation for worship.

At *St Christopher's* good quality taped music is relayed gently through he amplification system as the multi-cultural, mixed-age congregation take their seats. The choir is already seated five minutes before the service is advertised to begin. As soon as the taped music ceases the opening song of praise is announced and a well-ordered procession of crucifer, acolytes and two ministers enters the church. They process without fuss to their seats while the choir lead the congregation in the song. As soon as the song is finished a minister greets the people with a responsive sentence, announces the theme of the service, and invites the people to make their confession.

It is Pentecost at *St David's*, and the clergy and choir are hurrying to prepare for worship as the congregation arrive. The organist starts to play a dreary voluntary five minutes before the service is advertised to begin. Four minutes after the service should have begun the minister appears at the front of the church, nods at the organist to stop playing, welcomes everyone, and realizes that the amplification system is not working. Loud pitched feedback jolts everyone awake as the amplification comes to life. No-one can hear the announcement of the number of the opening processional hymn. Choir and clergy process slowly in a ragged crocodile to their seats. The minister turns and greets the people again – this time with a liturgical sentence. He then tells everyone to be seated and announces the notices for the week at some length, before inviting the congregation to join him in a prayer of preparation for worship.

Other options which *St Ann's* has used for Introductions include:

- Well-prepared notices, followed by the opening hymn and sentence/prayer of preparation.
- The giving of the Peace.
- A solo song or hymn.
- A spoken verse of a song or hymn.

On Palm Sunday, the people of *St Bartholomew's* take full advantage of the provision in *Lent, Holy Week, Easter*. They gather in the village hall for the greeting, invitation to worship, prayer over the palms, and a Gospel reading. Accompanied by the local band, they then process through the village, singing, to the church where the service continues with the collect and ministry of the Word.

2 Confessions

At *St Ann's* the deacon invites the congregation to kneel or sit in order to make their confession. Time is given for the people to settle down before the deacon invites the people to call to mind their sins against God and against their neighbour. After a time of silence for reflection, a sentence of Scripture is read aloud and the people are invited to confess their sins in the words of an authorized form of Confession from *Patterns for Worship*. The president prays for forgiveness using an authorized absolution in the 'us' form.

The Confession at *St Bartholomew's* during Holy Communion is said after the prayers of Intercession. The priest invites the people to sit or kneel and, after a pause, reads a seasonal sentence calling the people to repentance and to make their confession. As it is Lent, the responsive seasonal confession (2.3) from *Patterns for Worship* is used, the priest first reminding the congregation of the response: Lord, forgive: *Christ have mercy*. After the Confession, the priest pronounces the absolution. The congregation at *St Christopher's* remain standing for the Confession which takes place immediately after the Introduction to worship. It is Lent, and the prayers of penitence are introduced with the Summary of the Law, followed by a Kyrie Confession on the *Patterns for Worship* model, with appropriate insertions. At the absolution the sign of the cross is made by all, signalling their acceptance of God's forgiveness in Christ.

At *St David's* it is the monthly 'Family Service' and the minister has decided to use *Patterns for Worship* General Confession (2.10). No indication is given as to whether the congregation should sit or kneel and there is confusion as people look around to see what they should do. After a pause while the minister finds her service sheet, the people are asked to find their service sheets on which is printed the Confession. The minister invites the congregation to be quiet and to remember their sins before God in silence. She then immediately and loudly lists a number of sins on which the people may care to reflect and begins the confession, inserting these sins into it as she goes along. The absolution is mumbled inaudibly while the minister continues to kneel in her stall.

At *St Ann's* and *St Christopher's* several weeks are being devoted to teaching on repentance, confession and forgiveness. As a result their worship groups have recommended that the Confession be used at different times during various services:

- at ASB Rite A Holy Communion the Confession is normally near the beginning of the service, as part of the preparation for worship. Occasionally it now features after the Intercessions as part of the people's response in prayer to the Ministry of the Word.
- in services of the Word, Confession may be made:
  as a preparation for worship;
  as a response to the Word;
  towards the end of the service, as its climax.
- corporate preparation for confession may be made:
  in silence;
  whilst sentences or passages of Scripture are read aloud;
  during the singing of a suitable hymn or song, either corporately or by a solo voice.
- . . . and the *St Ann's* dance/drama group are looking at mime and other possibilities for expressing repentance and forgiveness . . .

3 The Word

People at *St Ann's* have done a lot of work on readings recently. The leadership group decided to have an adult teaching series on Romans, while the young people's groups continue with material based on the Gospel in the lectionary theme. As the children usually depart before the Gospel, and might not follow the long reading from Romans, the Gospel today comes immediately after the collect – everyone remains standing – and the children go out after the psalm that follows. The Gospel is the story of the breakfast on the seashore after the resurrection. It is read dramatically by well-rehearsed people from different parts of the building – the narrator at the lectern, Jesus by the communion table, and the disciples coming forward from the middle of the congregation.

For the sermon time, which lasts just over half an hour, the adults at St Ann's have a choice. Some go out to a discussion Bible study on Romans, others to a well-structured adult education session on the church and politics (linking up with Romans 13). The rest stay in church for a sermon on the same passage, with visuals on an overhead projector and questions at the end.

The four people who share the responsibility for reading at *St Bartholomew's* have recently been on a deanery training day for those who read, and as well as coming back with some good ideas for varying the usual pattern, are much more confident. There is a card on the lectern reminding the reader how to announce the reading. She introduces the reading with the paragraph heading and the page number from the pew Bible, and leaves space for some reflective silence before ending, 'This is the word of the Lord.'

At *St Christopher's* the worship committee has asked one or two artistic people in the church to produce something around the Gospel this Sunday. There is a throwover frontal on the altar, picking up the bread and fishes theme. The Gospel procession, with the deacon carrying the book of the Gospels, preceded by acolytes and crucifer, comes today only to the front row of the congregation. This is to keep people still facing towards the front, where on a screen behind the lectern there is a beautiful sequence of slides of Galilee, fishermen, bread and fishes. The sermon is about ten minutes long, and ends with some guided meditation inviting people to put themselves into the gospel story.

St Ann's worship group plans how the readings are done, usually a month at a time to make sure that there is variety and that the 'unusual' element is not overdone. Different methods they have used include:

- gentle musical backing to the reading, on tape or live;
- mime to the reading;
- especially at a family service, having the reading interrupted by someone asking questions, and putting in mistakes and asking the children to spot them;
- memorising a Gospel reading and telling it as a story declaiming one of the prophets, Amos for example, as if on a soap box.

The Sermon: what and where? The instructions for the Service of the Word redefine the sermon and outline different possibilities:

- more than one person taking part;
- the congregation dividing into groups for all (as at *St Ann's* here), or part of the time (for example, getting people talking to a couple of folk near them about how what is being said applies to them);
- the sermon in, say, two parts at different points in the service;
- time for silent – or guided reflection or meditation after the sermon.

Add to this some further things to consider:

- the use of handouts, either of the whole sermon or to help people take action;
- using overhead projector visuals in an integrated way, with pictures taking the application or story further, rather than merely summarising the sermon in words;
- sermons with deliberate interruptions and questions, or with pauses to pray or worship and sing;
- the use of drama, again as an integral part of the sermon.

Discussing these should open some new possibilities and also begin to answer the question 'Where?'. Clearly not all of these sermon activities are suitable for the pulpit. Different areas of the church may be used. And even with a more traditional sermon there may be a case for leaving the pulpit, moving nearer a small congregation at the back, walking up and down, speaking from the lectern where the word has been read, or from under a window whose stained glass enshrines the story . . .

The president at *St David's* sits for the first reading. No one comes forward to read so he glares at the churchwarden, moves to the lectern and intones the lesson in a voice betraying boredom. There is a bit of excitement, though, as – inevitably – two people come forward to read the second reading and look like having a punch up. The one who wins fails to announce where the reading comes from which is a pity as it seems to have been changed from what is on the notice sheet. It would have helped to be able to follow the reading, as he was speaking very quietly, on the mistaken assumption that the microphone was amplifying all he said. But no one had adjusted the height of it since one of the children read last Sunday.

4 Affirmation of Faith

At *St Ann's,* after the sermon, the preacher announces a reflective chorus, and encourages people to use it to make their response to the preaching. He then introduces the creed from the pulpit as the second part of their response. He uses the interrogative form of the creed from Resource Section 4, pointing out that the sermon was asking direct questions about their faith.

The sermon in *St Bartholomew's* (on today's theme of unity) mentions using the creed as a symbol of our unity in faith with the worldwide church through the ages. The Nicene Creed is introduced formally by the first four words,, without referring back to this. But it is clearly in the minds of many in church.

St Christopher's has recently been having some teaching on the creed. They have used one or two of the seasonal affirmations of faith in Resource Section 4 in *Patterns.* to fit with the teaching subject. One of the points that has been highlighted is the 'doxological' use of the creed in Eastern churches, to gather together the praise of the congregation. So today the creed is postponed until after the intercessions, when the choir lead an outburst of praise in a glorious setting of the Nicene Creed.

Meanwhile, in *St David's* the choir attempts to sing the Nicene Creed to a tune too difficult for them, let alone for the congregation to join in. They falter in the middle, miss a few words and have to start again. The congregation haven't been told how to occupy their time, and spend it meditating on the obvious disagreement between some of the choir and the clergy over which way to face while singing it – to the East for reverence to tradition, to the 'audience' for effect, or to one another, to keep in time . . . The creed does not appear to be fulfilling its function of uniting the church in the faith.

St Christopher's have had a debate about whether to use the Nicene Creed or the Apostles' Creed.

The Nicene Creed is traditional in communion and emphasises the corporate: '*We* believe'.

The Apostles' Creed has an individual emphasis, is shorter, and in easier language.

Both *St Ann's* and *St Bartholomew's* regularly use the Renewal of Baptismal Vows from the ASB at Easter and sometimes at New Year. Things have settled down now after the objections at *St Bartholomew's* because it was being used so frequently that it became meaningless.

What to use when from Resource Section 4

Affirmation 3 for the incarnation and Lent.
Affirmation 4 for the resurrection and memorial services.
Affirmation 5 for Advent, Trinity and heaven.
Affirmation 7 for the incarnation and Trinity.

8 Eucharistic Prayers

St Ann's celebrate a weekly Family communion service with children often present for the whole service. The eucharistic prayers in *Patterns for Worship* have been welcomed by the worship group as meeting their need for shorter, more responsive prayers. After discussion between the staff and worship group, the PCC have agreed that prayers C and D be used on a regular basis with a review on their use after six months. Prayers A and B will be introduced gradually, giving the congregation adequate time to learn the new prayers. The all-age learning groups in the church are following a course on 'The meal Jesus gives us' which includes teaching based on the new prayers.

The small congregation at *St Bartholomew's* is keen to use some of the new eucharistic material in *Patterns for Worship*. Their musical and printed resources are limited so the vicar opts initially to use prayer B with its regularly repeated congregational response which can be memorized. Seasonal and festive variety is provided by the president's 'triplet' insertions during the prayer. At the monthly 'Family Communion', attended by several families with toddlers, prayer D is used with a responsive thanksgiving preface (65.18) from *Patterns for Worship*.

The congregation at *St Christopher's* contains several people who find reading difficult and a group of children with hearing impediments. The eucharistic prayer is therefore often signed to the congregation, and much thought is given to the use of ceremonial and easily memorized musical settings. The provision for using well-known 'Sanctus'-type songs during the new eucharistic prayers is quickly adopted at *St Christopher's*. This they find particularly appropriate when using eucharistic prayer A. Sometimes a cantor is used to sing unfamiliar words which are then repeated by the congregation during the eucharistic prayer. This is very effective in prayer C, but works with other prayers as well.

The staff at *St David's* are delighted at the variety of eucharistic prayers which *Patterns for Worship* has on offer. It is decided to use a different prayer on each Sunday of the month (and on the 5th Sunday to revert to one of the Rite A prayers); 'we have got so bored with those long eucharistic prayers. . .' say the staff. Unfortunately on one Sunday the vicar forgets to print on the news-sheet the responsive thanksgiving preface which he has chosen as part of prayer D, and the congregation is excluded from effectively participating in the prayer. The following week (Palm

St Ann's discusses the eucharistic prayers

The *St Ann's* worship group considered a number of issues before deciding upon which eucharistic prayers to recommend for initial use, and when.

- The composition of the congregation in age and numbers.
- The ability of the congregation to learn and use new liturgical material.
- Having some services (with no children present?) when no books are used. This can easily be done with eucharistic prayers B and D, provided that the repeated response in B is not used.

The *St Ann's* music group are composing musical settings for the congregational words of the new eucharistic prayers.

The offertory at St Bartholomew's

At *St Bartholomew's* the preparation of the altar takes place during the singing of a hymn.

- The bread, wine and linen have been set ready beforehand on the credence table, and the president prepares the altar whilst the congregation sing.
- Sometimes a family prepares the altar, bringing the altar cloth, bread and wine from the credence table to the altar.
- The collection has been 'taken' in a basket with a notice on it, placed near the entrance as the congregation arrived for worship. During the offertory hymn, the basket is brought up to the altar by a member of the congregation and is presented by the president.
- By the end of the hymn, the altar has been prepared and the collection presented. The president begins the dialogue of the eucharistic prayer as soon as the hymn is finished.

Sunday) prayer B is used with 'triplet' insertions on the theme of the Resurrection. The last-minute production of the parish magazine has left the president no time to become acquainted with the full 'triplet' provision for prayer B, and he chooses the wrong set. After three months of the new prayers the PCC unanimously requests the vicar to revert to the BCP: 'at least we know where we are with the Book of Common Prayer!' growls one churchwarden.

At their Harvest agape *St Christopher's* used prayer A in the context of a bring-and-share meal.

Ceremonial at *St Christopher's* is kept simple but bold – the action and words of the eucharistic prayer complementing one another.

- the staff and worship group are looking at the question of whether some of the traditional ceremonial should be adapted and renewed in the light of the re-ordering of the church.

At *St Christopher's* the congregation have been taught unfamiliar responses in a variety of ways:

- repeating responses after a cantor during the service itself;
- producing a simple card with words and music available for any member of the congregation who wishes to use it;
- having a brief congregational rehearsal prior to the first service in which the responses were used. The congregation were invited a week beforehand to come to church ten minutes early the following week in order to learn the new material. A small group from the congregation met mid-week to prepare to lead the rehearsal.

APPENDIX 1: EXPLANATIONS

1 CONTENTS AND BACKGROUND

Contents *Patterns for Worship* consists of sample services suggested for publication as cards; service outlines; nine Resource Sections of liturgical texts; and guidance and advice about the conduct of Sunday worship. It seeks to respond to the needs of some parochial situations which are not adequately met by the provisions of the Book of Common Prayer or the Alternative Service Book. These include the need to provide for worship in Family Services and in Urban Priority Areas, specifically referred to the Liturgical Commission by the House of Bishops.

Consultation and experiment There has been extensive consultation in UPAs in different parts of the country, with Diocesan Liturgical Committee secretaries, with members of the Black Anglican Concerns Committee, with the RSCM, the Council for the Deaf, and the Adult Education Committee of the Board of Education, among others. Some of the material has already been in use (where necessary under the provisions of Canon B 5A). *Patterns for Worship* should be viewed as part of the continuing process of exploration by which the Church seeks to discern what forms of worship should be authorized after 2000. Neither the House of Bishops nor the Liturgical Commission should assume that every development suggested here will prove successful or acceptable. Only by a process of exploration and reflection will the Church be able to assess adequately what texts and approaches are of lasting value. Therefore any legal authorization needed should expire by the year 2000.

2 AUTHORIZATION

Synodical authorization under the full Liturgical Business procedure would be necessary for:

1 A Form of Service for Morning or Evening Prayer: The Service of the Word

2 A Form of Service for The Holy Communion (Rite C)

3 Alternative Confessions and Absolutions (Resource Section 2)

4 Alternative Eucharistic Prayers (Resource Section 9)

The remainder of the material in *Patterns for Worship* could initially be commended by the House of Bishops under Canon B 4, following a Synod debate and revision by the Liturgical

Commission, in the same way as *Lent, Holy Week, Easter*, but would eventually be largely covered by the authorization of the two services above.

When *Patterns for Worship* is introduced to the Synod, the Chairman of the Commission will invite members of the Synod to say if they feel strongly that any other area in *Patterns for Worship*, for example the Affirmations of Faith, should go through the full Liturgical Business procedure. Some ways of approaching some of the potential 'problem areas' can be seen from the questions that follow. Question 2, in particular, deals with local authorization.

3 QUESTIONS, AND SOME GUIDELINES ON APPROACHING THEM

It may be helpful to have some suggested answers to questions people ask on liturgical matters, both as regards the ASB and on the position if and when *Patterns for Worship* is approved by the Synod. They have been compiled by the Liturgical Commission, with the approval of the Legal Adviser.

1 Do these proposals undermine Common Prayer in the Church of England?

It may help to identify three aspects of the Anglican understanding of common prayer.

First, the valuing of patterns of worship which are recognized as the common possession of the people of God. This does not mean that nothing can change nor that every popular practice must prevail. It does not rule out any local variation. It does mean that worship must not simply be governed by the whim of the minister or the congregation. Corporate patterns of worship must exist and be developed which are recognized by worshippers as their corporate worship. It is therefore appropriate that these are approved and regulated by the Church.

Second, the patterns and forms of worship must not be determined purely at the level of the local congregation but must bear witness to participation in the wider common life of the Church. For this reason it is right that common forms of e.g. creeds, collects, confessions, and eucharistic prayers should be followed, as well as common approaches to the shape and content of Christian worship.

Third, patterns of common prayer play an important part in maintaining the unity of the Church in its confession of the Christian faith. For this reason:

(a) those authorized to lead worship promise 'to use only the forms of service which are authorized or allowed by canon';

(b) while ministers have considerable liturgical freedom under Canon B 5, they are charged to ensure such services are 'neither contrary to, nor indicative of any departure from, the doctrine of the Church of England in any essential matter'. The same provision applies to services derived from *Patterns for Worship*.

(c) General Synod in recent years has taken great care that all liturgical forms it has authorized can be used with a good conscience by the different traditions in the Church of England. In compiling *Patterns for Worship* the Liturgical Commission, which is widely representative of the different traditions, has taken similar care. The same care to respect others' traditions should be taken by those who compile services from the *Patterns for Worship* provisions.

2 Who has the authority to change the worship in our parish church?

There is a good description of the present legal position on this in *Public Worship in the Church of England*. The provisions of Canon B 3 will apply to the forms of service in *Patterns for Worship*, once they are authorized by the Synod. This means in general that decisions as to which forms of service are used are taken jointly by the minister and the PCC. In cases of disagreement, the BCP or a form previously in use for two of the past four years is to be used. There is no provision for appeal to the bishop under Canon B 3, apart from cases where there is dispute over the form to be used for occasional offices. Matters under Canon B 5 can be referred to the bishop, where there is doubt about whether a variation in a service made by the minister is of substantial importance or not.

But the spirit of the Worship and Doctrine Measure is that there should be agreement at local level. The procedure of Section 1 (3) of the Worship and Doctrine Measure (1974) should be followed. The PCC should have full discussion and agreement on these questions:

(a) How often is *The Service of the Word* or *The Holy Communion (Rite C)* to be used? Is there to be, say, a monthly pattern which will involve the use of the Book of Common Prayer or the Alternative Service Book?

(b) Does the PCC want to put specific limitations on the contents of either service?

(c) For what period of time will the PCC agree to *The Service of the Word* or *The Holy Communion (Rite C)* being used? When will the PCC review this pattern of worship?

If the bishop or his representative is involved either in an advisory capacity or on appeal, he should ask for a report stating that these provisions have been followed.

3 'Please will you authorize this eucharistic prayer for use with children in our church school?'

It does not matter legally whether the service is in school or in church. Canon B 1 limits Church of England ministers to using only the services it covers, unless it is claimed that the provisions of Canon B 5 apply, namely that it is a service for which no provision is made in the Book of Common Prayer or under Canons B 2 or B 4. Our common understanding is that Canon B 5 cannot be stretched to cover services of Holy Communion even if they are for specific occasions, age groups, or places not specifically provided for in the BCP or Canons B2 and B 4. So a service of Holy Communion for St Swithun's Day should be regarded primarily as a service of Holy Communion (and therefore coming under Canons B 1 and B 2), and not as a special liturgy for St Swithun (for which the BCP etc. makes no provision, thus leaving the minister to his own discretion under Canon B 5).

4 May I use different forms of confession and invitation to confession in Holy Communion?

Rite A, Section 6, allows 'other suitable words' to be used for the invitation to confession. We generally take the words in brackets '(see section 25)' as a helpful cross-reference, rather than as having the effect of restricting alternatives to those in Section 25. The rubrics in *The Service of the Word* and *The Holy Communion (Rite C)*, and the provisions in Resource Section 2, in *Patterns for Worship*, regularize this position, extend the option of using other suitable words to Morning and Evening Prayer, and provide examples of such words.

We have generally not taken 'other suitable words' in Rite A, Section 6, to refer also to the form of confession, though we accept that it is ambiguous, and that the rubric at Section 4 says 'Alternative confessions may be used.' We have generally seen these alternatives as being limited to those in Rite A, Section 80. *Patterns for Worship* makes it clear that only authorized forms of confession may be used, and extends very slightly the range of confessions available.

5 May I use a credal hymn instead of the Nicene Creed in the Holy Communion?

It is important for our unity in the catholic faith that any creeds used are not private or local compositions, but ones that are recognized by the wider Church. However, both in ASB Morning and Evening Prayer and in Rite A Holy Communion the creed may be omitted on weekdays, so it clearly does not make the service invalid in some way. And it is true that public recitation of the creed has not always been an essential part of the Church's worship. *Patterns for Worship* allows for the occasional omission of the creed, provided it is replaced by one of the Affirmations of Faith in Resource Section 4. A glance at these will show that they largely consist of material already authorized, dialogue and catechetical versions of the creeds, some scripture excerpts for seasonal use, and a version of part of the Athanasian Creed. There is no provision for the use of a credal hymn as a substitute.

APPENDIX 2 MATTERS OF DOCTRINE

1 Canon A 5, Of the Doctrine of the Church of England, states:

> 'The doctrine of the Church of England is grounded in the Holy Scriptures, and in such teachings of the ancient Fathers and Councils of the Church as are agreeable to the said Scriptures. In particular such doctrine is to be found in the Thirty-nine Articles of Religion, the Book of Common Prayer, and the Ordinal.'

This canon is entrenched in the Worship and Doctrine Measure 1974 (5(1)). It is under this Measure that alternative forms of service to the Book of Common Prayer and new forms of declaration of assent for church office holders have been authorized.

2 The Worship and Doctrine Measure 1974 requires that 'every form of service . . . approved by the General Synod . . . shall be such as in the opinion of the General Synod is neither contrary to, nor indicative of any departure from, the doctrine of the Church of England in any essential matter'. (S4(1)). S4(2) states: 'The final approval of the General Synod of any such Canon or regulation or form of service or amendment thereof shall conclusively determine that the Synod is of such opinion as aforesaid with respect to the matter so approved.'

3 In considering whether any rite is contrary to, or indicative of any departure from, the doctrine of the Church of England in any essential matter, reference should be made to:

i the Holy Scriptures

ii such teachings of the Fathers and the Councils of the Church as are agreeable to the said Scriptures

iii the Thirty-nine Articles of Religion, the Book of Common Prayer and the Ordinal of 1662

iv such forms of service, canons and regulations as have received the final approval of General Synod.

Attention will need to be paid to (iv) in weighing matters that have recently been in dispute in the Church of England. Where, in controversial matters, General Synod has taken care not to depart from the teachings or usage found in (iii), this should be respected.

A NOTE ON NUMBERING

In the longer Resource Sections of *Patterns for Worship,* a three-part system of numbering is used. This consists of an italic number, followed by two ordinary numbers separated by a full point : e.g. *7* 52.17

The middle number identifies the particular Resource Section and any subsection within it.

Thus 5 = Prayer. 52 = Post-Communion Prayers and Endings for Word Services.

The last number is a continuous numbering within the Section or subsection.

The first, italic number indicates the theme or season, e.g. *7* for Ascension, Kingship.

Items for a particular theme or season can be found by looking for the first number : see Index of Themes and Seasons below.

Only the middle and the last number appear in the Index of Scripture References which follows.

INDEX OF THEMES AND SEASONS

1 Advent
2 Incarnation, Christmas, Annunciation, Mary
3 Epiphany, Light
4 Lent, Penitence
5 Cross
6 Resurrection, Heaven, Glory, Transfiguration, Death, Funerals
7 Ascension, Kingship
8 Spirit, Pentecost, Gifts, Healing, Baptism and Confirmation
9 Creation, Harvest, Bread, Vine
10 Word
11 Church, Mission and Ministry, Unity
12 City, World and Society
13 Family
14 Saints (See also Resurrection)
15 Kingdom, Freedom, Reconciliation
16 Love, Peace, Joy
17 General, Extempore Examples

INDEX OF SCRIPTURE REFERENCES